FORTRESS • 105

FORTS OF THE AMERICAN FRONTIER 1776–1891

California, Oregon, Washington, and Alaska

RON FIELD

ILLUSTRATED BY ADAM HOOK

Series editor Marcus Cowper

First published in 2011 by Osprey Publishing
Midland House, West Way, Botley, Oxford OX2 0PH, UK
44-02 23rd St, Suite 219, Long Island City, NY 11101, USA

E-mail: info@ospreypublishing.com

A CIP catalog record for this book is available from the British Library.

Print ISBN: 978 1 84908 315 7
PDF e-book ISBN: 978 1 84908 316 4
EPUB e-book ISBN: 978 1 84908 883 1

Editorial by Ilios Publishing Ltd, Oxford, UK (www.iliospublishing.com)
Cartography: The Map Studio
Page layout by Ken Vail Graphic Design, Cambridge, UK (kvgd.com)
Index by David Worthington
Originated by United Graphic Pte Ltd.
Printed in China through Bookbuilders

11 12 13 14 15   10 9 8 7 6 5 4 3 2 1

Osprey Publishing are supporting the Woodland Trust, the UK's leading woodland conservation charity, by funding the dedication of trees.

www.ospreypublishing.com

ACKNOWLEDGMENTS

My thanks go to Robin J. Wellman, Interpretative Specialist, Russian River District, Fort Ross State Historic Park; Susan Snyder, Head of Public Services, The Bancroft Library, University of California; Laura Mulholland, Special Collections Division, University of Washington Libraries, Seattle; Carolyn Marr, Librarian, Museum of History & Industry, Seattle; Fred Poyner IV, Registrar & Digital Assets Manager, Washington State Historical Society; Scott Rook, Digital Assets Manager, Oregon Historical Society; and Todd Kepple, Manager, Klamath County Museum, Oregon.

ARTIST'S NOTE

Readers may care to note that the original paintings from which the color plates in this book were prepared are available for private sale. All reproduction copyright whatsoever is retained by the Publishers. All enquiries should be addressed to:

Scorpio Gallery, PO Box 475, Hailsham, East Sussex BN27 2SL, UK

The Publishers regret that they can enter into no correspondence upon this matter.

THE FORTRESS STUDY GROUP (FSG)

The object of the FSG is to advance the education of the public in the study of all aspects of fortifications and their armaments, especially works constructed to mount or resist artillery. The FSG holds an annual conference in September over a long weekend with visits and evening lectures, an annual tour abroad lasting about eight days, and an annual Members' Day.

The FSG journal FORT is published annually, and its newsletter Casemate is published three times a year. Membership is international. For further details, please contact:

secretary@fsgfort.com
Website: www.fsgfort.com

THE HISTORY OF FORTIFICATION STUDY CENTER (HFSC)

The History of Fortification Study Center (HFSC) is an international scientific research organization that aims to unite specialists in the history of military architecture from antiquity to the 20th century (including historians, art historians, archeologists, architects and those with a military background). The center has its own scientific council, which is made up of authoritative experts who have made an important contribution to the study of fortification.

The HFSC's activities involve organizing conferences, launching research expeditions to study monuments of defensive architecture, contributing to the preservation of such monuments, arranging lectures and special courses in the history of fortification and producing published works such as the refereed academic journal Questions of the History of Fortification, monographs and books on the history of fortification. It also holds a competition for the best publication of the year devoted to the history of fortification.

The headquarters of the HFSC is in Moscow, Russia, but the Center is active in the international arena and both scholars and amateurs from all countries are welcome to join. More detailed information about the HFSC and its activities can be found on the website: www.hfsc.3dn.ru

E-mail: ciif-info@yandex.ru

MEASUREMENT CONVERSIONS

Imperial measurements are used throughout this book. The following data will help in converting the imperial measurements to metric.

1 mile = 1.6km
1lb = 0.45kg
1oz = 28g
1 yard = 0.9m
1ft = 0.3m
1in. = 2.54cm/25.4mm
1 gal = 4.5 liters
1pt = 0.47 liters
1 ton (US) = 0.9 tonnes
1hp = 0.745kW

CONTENTS

FORTS OF THE AMERICAN FRONTIER 1776–1891

INTRODUCTION

The first fortifications on the Pacific Coast of the North American continent were built by Native Americans. Ancient strongpoints in Alaska, such as Grouse Fort in Ground Hog Bay, and Brown Bear Fort on Admiralty Island, existed long before European exploration began. The first European peoples to establish fortifications on the West Coast were the Russians. In 1639 their explorers reached the Pacific through Siberia and by the 1770s the Russian Fur Company, chartered by the tsarist government to control all exploration, trade, and settlement in the North Pacific, had created a profitable fur trade in Alaska. By the early 1800s the Russian–American Company was exporting an average of 62,000 fur pelts per annum. In 1799 company manager Alexander Baranov established a fortified trade factory called Fort Archangel Gabriel in Sitka Bay, Alaska. The first permanent Russian trade fort in California was built in 1812 by Ivan Kuskov. Established on the coast of what is today Sonoma County, Fort Ross became the site of the first windmills and shipbuilding in California, and Russian scientists were among the first to record the cultural and natural history of the area. The post was a successfully functioning multi-cultural settlement for about 30 years, with a population including Russians, Native Alaskans, Californians, and Creoles (of mixed Russian and native ancestry).

This general view of Fort Ross was produced around the year 1840, and shows the two seven-sided blockhouses in opposite corners and the chapel at the center. (Library of Congress, HABS CAL, 49-FORO, 1–5)

The major forts, camps, and blockhouses on the West Coast, 1776–1891

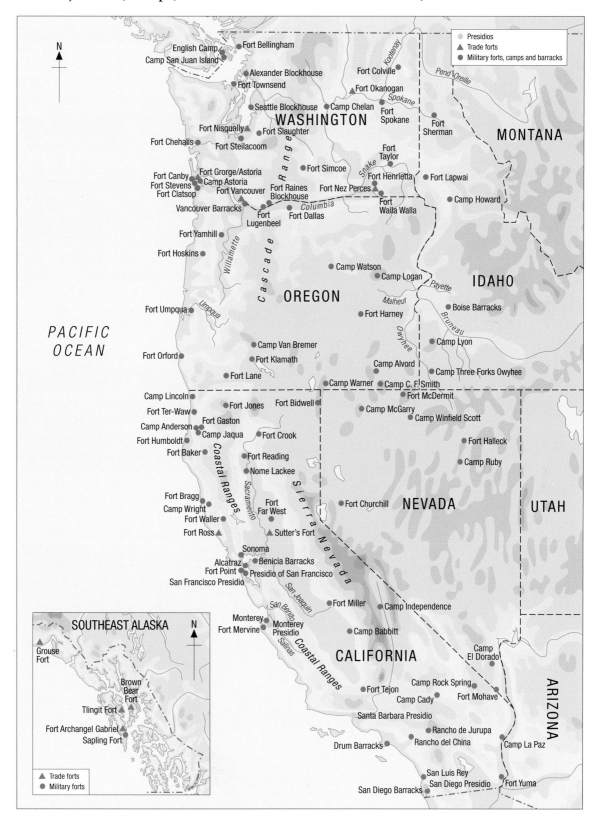

N

Presidios
Trade forts
Military forts, camps and barracks

Fort Bellingham
English Camp
Camp San Juan Island
Fort Colville
Kootenay
Pend Oreille
MONTANA

Alexander Blockhouse
Fort Townsend
Fort Okanogan
Spokane

Seattle Blockhouse
Camp Chelan
Fort Spokane
Fort Sherman

WASHINGTON
Fort Nisqually
Fort Slaughter
Fort Steilacoom
Fort Chehalis
Range
Fort Taylor
Fort Simcoe
Snake
Fort Henrietta
Fort Lapwai

Fort Canby
Fort Grorge/Astoria
Camp Astoria
Fort Stevens
Fort Vancouver
Fort Clatsop
Fort Raines
Blockhouse
Fort Nez Perces
Camp Howard

Vancouver Barracks
Columbia
Fort
Walla Walla

Fort
Lugenbeel
Fort Dallas

Fort Yamhill
Cascade
Willamette

Fort Hoskins
Camp Watson
Camp Logan
Payette
IDAHO

OREGON
Malheur
Boise Barracks

Fort Umpqua
Umpqua
Fort Harney
Bruneau

PACIFIC
OCEAN
Owyhee
Camp Lyon

Camp Van Bremer
Camp Alvord
Camp Three Forks Owyhee

Fort Orford
Fort Klamath
Camp Warner
Camp C. F. Smith

Fort Lane
Fort McDermit

Camp Lincoln
Fort Jones
Fort Bidwell
Camp McGarry

Fort Ter-Waw
Fort Gaston
Camp Winfield Scott

Camp Anderson
Camp Jaqua
Fort Crook

Fort Humboldt
Fort Halleck

Fort Baker
Fort Reading
Camp Ruby

Nome Lackee

Coastal Ranges
Sierra Nevada

Fort Bragg
Camp Wright
Fort
Far West
Fort Churchill
NEVADA
UTAH

Fort Waller
Sacramento

Fort Ross
Sutter's Fort

Sonoma

Alcatraz
Benicia Barracks
Fort Point
Presidio of San Francisco
San Francisco Presidio

San Joaquin
Fort Miller
Camp Independence

Monterey
Monterey
Presidio
San Benito
Camp Babbitt

Fort Mervine
Salinas
Camp
El Dorado

CALIFORNIA
Coastal Ranges
Camp Rock Spring
Fort Tejon
Fort Mohave
Camp Cady
ARIZONA

Santa Barbara Presidio
Rancho de Jurupa
Rancho del China
Camp La Paz

Drum Barracks

San Luis Rey
San Diego Presidio
Fort Yuma
San Diego Barracks

SOUTHEAST ALASKA

N

Grouse
Fort

Brown
Bear
Fort

Tlingit Fort

Fort Archangel Gabriel
Sapling Fort

Trade forts
Military forts

A Spanish presence on the West Coast from the 17th century led to several claims on California, as this mighty colonial power sought to consolidate its position in North America. Recognizing the significance of a vast harbor in what became known as San Francisco Bay, Spain began to fortify the area. Construction of the first defenses there began in 1776 when a lightly fortified military outpost known as El Presidio de San Francisco was built just inside the Golden Gate to provide protection for the garrisoned soldiers. This fortification and others at San Diego, Monterey, and Santa Barbara were largely constructed using labor provided by indigenous peoples.

The first United States fort in the Far West, Fort Clatsop was established by Meriwether Lewis and William Clark in 1805 in what became Oregon Territory. It had taken the intrepid pioneers 18 months to travel over 4,000 miles (6,440km) overland to the Pacific, where they waited out the cold winter of 1805–06 before returning east. Five years later John Jacob Astor's Pacific Fur Company built a stockade trading post nearby, originally called Fort Astoria, then Fort George, and reverting later to Fort Astoria. As the Treaty of 1818 permitted joint occupancy of Oregon Country by the US and Great Britain, the British-owned Hudson's Bay Company, which merged with the North West Company in 1821, went on to build and operate at least 23 forts and five trading stations at the height of its power during the first half of the 19th century. This company's stranglehold on the region was loosened and finally broken following the first successful large wagon train to reach Oregon in 1843.

In 1846 the Oregon Treaty finally brought to an end the boundary dispute between the US and Great Britain, and the 49th parallel became the border between the territories of the two nations. The acquisition of Oregon Country in the north was balanced in the south by the Mexican cession of 1848. The Mexican–American War of 1846–48, followed by the acquisition of California and New Mexico by the US, was a major turning point in the development of the western military frontier. These newly acquired areas opened up a vast new region to American settlement. The westward movement to California and Oregon, as well as to Texas and the Rio Grande Valley in New Mexico, called for increased military protection from Federal troops. However, problems involved in establishing and maintaining these frontier outposts were multiplied by the fact that they were no longer on the edge of areas of settlement easily accessed by the river system of the eastern United States. At vast distances from sources of supply, and in remote areas where few local resources were available, these posts made serious demands on the US War Department.

The movement westward of emigrants to Oregon had been steady throughout the 1840s, and settlements along the Columbia River had already sprung up. For the protection of these citizens, troops were placed on the Columbia River. Vancouver Barracks was established near the site of the Hudson's Bay Company post in May 1849, while Camp Astoria was built at the mouth of the river the same year, and Camp Drum was located at the gorge of the river in May 1850. While these garrisons protected the western end of the Oregon Trail, additional troops guarded it along the way from Missouri.

During the 1850s the US Army shifted its main effort to the area west of the 98th meridian as increased activity among settlers, emigrants, and miners stirred up hostility among the Native American peoples. The further influx of newcomers into California after the discovery of gold at Sutter's Mill in 1848 caused widespread tension, as they seemed determined to grab everything in

Described as "one of the prettiest and most attractive military stations on the Pacific slope," Fort Klamath was originally established as a two-company post in 1863. The whitewashed wood-frame buildings surrounding the parade ground are seen behind these cavalry troopers. (Courtesy of the Fort Klamath Museum)

the territory for themselves. Hence, the Native Americans often became hostile in an attempt to preserve their lands and identity. As a result the War Department dotted California with forts, which defended settlements on the coast or protected mining communities in "Gold Country." Garrisons were also placed along the routes of communication, in order to protect traffic going to and from the gold mines.

The Gold Rush also heightened the need for strong fortifications elsewhere on the coastline. Not only was the wealth of the gold fields incalculable, but also maritime traffic into San Francisco increased dramatically, with 770 vessels visiting the port in 1849. The following year a joint Army–Navy board recommended the construction of two major forts, one on either shore of the Golden Gate straits formed by Fort Point and Lime Point. Although work on the former was begun by 1853, long litigation for acquisition of land prevented commencement of the latter, which became known as Fort Baker, until the 1890s. Backing up these outer defense works would be an inner system consisting of a third major fort on Alcatraz Island, which would be supported by smaller batteries on Angel Island, Yerba Buena Island, and Point San Jose on the northern San Francisco waterfront.

During the same period of the mid-1850s, disturbances among the Native American peoples in Washington Territory required a stronger military presence in the Pacific Northwest. Continued friction caused by the migration of settlers and miners into that region led to a general outbreak of hostilities in 1855–56, known as the Yakima War, which led to the creation of a number of important military posts, as well as blockhouses along the Cascades of the Columbia River.

Triggered by the shooting of a pig but in reality a longer-term dispute between the US and the British Empire regarding an international boundary, the Pig War of 1859 led to the construction of blockhouses and earthworks on San Juan Island. Although the Civil War that raged from 1861–65 diverted attention from the frontier, it did not remove the duty to protect the western population from hostile Native Americans, who took advantage of the Union's preoccupation with the struggle against the Confederacy. While fighting took place in the Border States and the South, the Army posts on the Pacific Coast were required to carry on their essential function. Mostly garrisoned by volunteer forces, which replaced US regulars, campaigns were conducted against the Paiutes east of the Cascade Mountains in Oregon and in the Owens Valley in California, and against the Bannock and Shoshone in Washington Territory.

This view looking across the estuary towards the Presidio de San Carlos de Monterey was produced by British artist Richard Brydges Beechey when he was a midshipman aboard HMS *Blossom*, around 1826. His vessel can be seen in the far-right background. (Courtesy of The Bancroft Library)

As the immigrant and mining population continued to increase after the Civil War, so did the need for their protection. By 1875 a total of 13 posts, including Alcatraz Island and Benicia Barracks, were garrisoned by the regular Army in the Department of California, while a further 11 posts served the Department of the Columbia in Washington Territory and Oregon. The Modoc War of 1873 in California, and intermittent warfare with the Bannock and Paiute in eastern Oregon during 1879, resulted in the last major period of conflict with Native Americans on the West Coast.

CHRONOLOGY

1769	Establishment of the Spanish Presidio of San Diego, the first permanent European settlement on the Pacific Coast.
1781	Yuma Revolt.
1784	First permanent Russian colony in Alaska founded by Grigory Shelikhov.
1802	Fort Archangel Gabriel in Alaska captured by the Tlingit people.
1805	Lewis and Clark expedition reaches Oregon Country.
1818	Treaty of 1818 permits the joint occupancy of Oregon Country by the US and Great Britain.
1819	French-Argentine privateer Hipólito de Bouchard attacks Spanish possessions on the California coast.
1825	Merger of Hudson's Bay Company and North West Company.
1846–48	Mexican–American War.
1848–55	California Gold Rush.
1850	California admitted to the Union as the 31st state.
1850	Army–Navy Board recommends the fortification of San Francisco Harbor.
1850–51	Mariposa War.
1853	Construction of Fort Point begins.
1855–56	Rogue River War.
1855–58	Yakima War.
1856	"Cascades Massacre."
1859–72	Pig War, or Northwestern Boundary Dispute, between the US and Great Britain on San Juan Island.
1859	Oregon admitted to the Union as the 33rd state.
1861–65	American Civil War.
1862	California Column marches 900 miles (1,450km) to western Texas.
1864	Snake War.

1867	Alaska sold to the US for 7.2 million dollars.
1871	Treaty of Washington between the US and Great Britain.
1873	Modoc War.
1889	Washington admitted to the Union as the 42nd state.

DEVELOPMENT OF THE FORTS

Native American fortifications

Explorers who visited the Northwest Coast during the 18th century noted various fortified rocks and headlands. While investigating Kalinin Bay, in Salisbury Sound, Sitka territory, as part of the second expedition ordered by Antonio María de Bucareli y Ursú, Viceroy of New Spain, in August, 1775, the pilot aboard the ship *Sonora* wrote, "we saw, on the bank of the river, a high house, and a parapet of timber supported by stakes drove into the ground, where we observed ten Indian men, besides women and children." In 1794, Captain George Vancouver, of the British Royal Navy, observed in detail eight defensive positions near the entrance to Kake Strait, at Hamilton Bay, on Kupreanof Island, stating, "These fortified places were well constructed with a strong platform of wood, laid on the most elevated part of the rock, and projecting so as to overspread the declivity. The edge of the platform was surrounded by a barricade raised by logs of wood placed on each other."

The fort built by the Tlingit people after they had destroyed Fort Archangel Gabriel (see "The forts at war") and temporarily driven the Russians out of the Sitka area in 1802 was described by Yuri Lisiansky, captain of the ship *Neva*, as "an irregular square, its longest side looking towards the sea. It was constructed of wood so strong, that the shot from my guns could not penetrate it at the short distance of a cable's length [100–120 fathoms, which was 608ft or 185m]." According to a drawing produced by Lisiansky, this fort had two embrasures for cannon, and was "an irregular parallelogram, about one hundred fathoms, or six hundred feet long in the largest dimension; the lower part of the walls was made of four courses of horizontal logs, above which rose a palisade of vertical logs set close together. The latter were connected near their tops, on the outside only, by a horizontal beam, and braced at intervals by posts on the outside, leaning against the wall."

Forced out of Norfolk Sound by the Russians in 1804, the Tlingit people fortified themselves at Point Hayes, on the southeastern shore of Chichagof Island, where German-born explorer George Heinrich Von Langsdorff observed they had fortified themselves upon "a rock which rises perpendicularly to the heighth of some hundred feet above the water... The rock itself is secured against the attack of an enemy by a double palisade of large tree trunks stuck close together, measuring twelve to fifteen feet in heighth, and from three to four feet in thickness. A high natural wall of earth beyond the palisading, on the side towards the sea, conceals the habitations effactually, so that they cannot be discerned by any ship."

As recently as April 1869, soldiers aboard the US steamer *Saginaw*, commanded by Captain Richard W. Meade, destroyed two forts and several villages of the Kake people in Security Bay on Kuiu Island in retaliation for the murder of two American hunters. The Kake forts were described

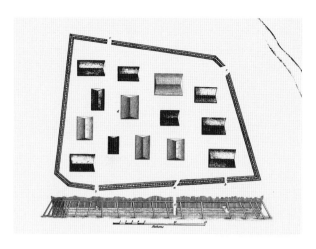

Based on a sketch made in 1804 by Russian explorer Yuri Lisiansky, this engraving shows the Tlingit "Sapling Fort," on Baranov Island, Alaska. According to Lisiansky, it was "constructed of wood, so thick and strong," that the shot from his guns could not penetrate it "at the short distance of a cable's length." (*A Voyage Around the World*, 1814)

as stockades "about 100ft square and from 15 to 17 feet high, and built from logs from 9 to 15 inches thick."

Trade and supply forts

Few ventures were more profitable than the fur trade on the North American continent during the first half of the 19th century. Otter and beaver pelts sold for high prices in the Far East, and beaver hats were fashionable in both Europe and America. By land and sea, Russian, American, British, and Canadian traders came into the Northwest to carry valuable beaver furs all over the world. The Native Americans provided the majority of the pelts to the traders, and posts were set up in the wilderness to attract their trade. Not only was the fur trade an important business, it also featured prominently in securing the Northwest for the US rather than for Canada.

The Russian presence in Alaska eventually resulted in the establishment of several substantial trade forts. Built in 1800 near modern-day Sitka under the supervision of Alexander Baranov, Fort Archangel Gabriel was protected by 32 cannon and consisted of "a strong two-story building, guarded by a palisade and two [octagonal] blockhouses." Earlier in the 1790s, Fort St Alexander had consisted of a "square, with bastions at two of the corners, and … a gate protected by two guns." A blockhouse and stockade also existed at Yakutat, for the protection of Siberian settlers in the employ of the Russian-American Company.

Established in California in 1812 and named after *Rossiia* (Russia), Fort Ross was the southernmost outpost of the Russian presence in North America. The Russians remained at Fort Ross until the year 1841. Visiting the post in 1822, Father Mariano Payéras described it as being "situated atop a mesa which is surrounded by ravines which abut the sea. It is constructed of redwood planks (there is no other wood used in any of the structures) and forms a palisade. It is four varas [33in., or 84cm] high, uniformly, and is surmounted by a beam set with pointed stakes intended to dissuade any assault. It has three gates: one to the northeast, one to the west and one to the southeast." Reporting to Governor José Figueroa, commander of the Presidio of San Francisco, in 1833, Mariano Vallejo stated that its "walls form a quadrangle of exactly 100 varas [275ft, or 84m] square." The formidable appearance of Fort Ross was enhanced by a seven-sided blockhouse in the northwest corner and an eight-sided one in the southeast corner, plus sentries on the two corners without blockhouses, "from which the sentinels chime bells each hour." The former blockhouse protected access from the sea and the latter from the road. As a result of these defense works, erected against the natives and Spanish, the cannon were never fired in anger. Inside the stockade stood "the commander's house, two warehouses … another warehouse filled with provisions for the fort; a barracks and three officials' houses." In case of siege, a "draw-well" was dug inside the stockade.

Like Fort Ross, most of the trade forts built by the Hudson's Bay Company, appears to have been based on a simple plan consisting of a stockade encompassing a compound, with blockhouses or bastions at two opposite corners to provide flanking fire along its four walls. The stockade

This reconstruction of the west gate at Fort Ross shows the palisade of redwood planks topped by a beam "set with pointed stakes intended to dissuade any assault." (Courtesy of California State Parks, 2010)

constructed usually consisted of logs prepared as pickets by being sharpened to a point at one end. Alternatively sharpened on the thin and thick ends, when placed side by side in the palisade with the sharpened ends up these logs would fit together without significant gaps. At many Company posts it was normal procedure to square two sides of the log so that the pickets would butt together more evenly. In order to prevent rotting once set into the ground, the base of each main support post was stripped of its bark and charred thoroughly on the outside. After the posts were raised, it was the usual practice of the Hudson's Bay Company to attach them to cross pieces that ran horizontally around the inside of the wall about 4ft (1.2m) from the top. The pickets were secured to this girth with wooden pegs or by means of an "oblique notch." The ends of the cross pieces, which were about 15ft (4.5m) long, were mortised into larger pickets called "king posts." The gates installed were cut out of the palisade wall, and the pickets continued in an uninterrupted row across the top of each gateway opening. The actual gates were about 6–7in. (15–18cm) thick and heavily studded with large nails, and usually had a small wicket, or door, cut into them so that a single person or a small party could enter without making it necessary to open the entire gate.

Originally named Fort George, Fort Astoria was established at the mouth of the mighty Columbia River by Jacob Astor's Pacific Fur Company in 1811. Situated only about 5 miles (8km) northwest of the site of the abandoned Fort Clatsop, built by explorers Lewis and Clark in 1805 (see below), Fort

A Russian-style chapel stands in the mist surrounding Fort Ross in northern California. It was restored following damage sustained during the 1906 earthquake, and is today called the Holy Trinity Chapel. (Courtesy of California State Parks, 2010)

Astoria was sold to the British-owned North West Company in 1813 and served as the company headquarters of that organization until 1821, and as the regional depot of the Columbia District of the Hudson's Bay Company after the merger of 1825. Although the British maintained control of this fort until October 6, 1818, on which date it was turned over to the US, it continued as a British-occupied post. Fort Astoria was linked to the east via river and overland with the York Factory on Hudson Bay, and thence to London, England. It was described by William Henry Gray, who reached the post with the Whitman party of missionaries in the fall of 1836, as consisting of "a stockade made of fir-logs, twenty feet high above the ground, inclosing

Produced soon after Fort Astoria was established in 1811, this engraving shows the solid stockade walls and bastions that provided the defenses for this Pacific Fur Company trading post. (University of Washington Libraries, Special Collections Division)

a parallelogram of one hundred and fifty by two hundred and fifty feet, extending in its greatest length from northwest to southeast, and defended by bastions, or towers, at two opposite angles." Within this enclosure were all the buildings of the establishment. The Indian Hall or trading shop, plus storehouses, formed the east side of the court, while the officers' dwelling and the shelters for the servants ranged along the north and west sides. The fort was protected by artillery consisting of two heavy 18-pdrs, six 6-pdrs, four 4-pdrs, two 6-pdr coehorn mortars, and seven swivel-guns, all mounted.

Also originally established by the Pacific Fur Company at the confluence of the Okanogan and Columbia rivers in 1811, Fort Okanogan was the first American-owned settlement in what is now Washington State. In 1816 it was rebuilt under the supervision of Irishman Ross Cox, who recorded in his journal:

> By the month of September we had erected a new dwelling house for the person in charge, containing four excellent rooms and a large dining hall, two good houses for the men and a spacious store for the furs and merchandise to which was attached a shop for trading with the natives. The whole was surrounded by strong palisades fifteen feet high and flanked by two bastions. Each bastion had in its lower story a light brass four pounder, and the upper loopholes were left for the use of musketry.

As the landing site on the Okanogan was too shallow and the banks too steep, the post was abandoned and rebuilt nearer the Columbia River sometime between 1831 and 1837. With the ratification of the Oregon Treaty in 1846, which ended the Oregon boundary dispute and the joint-occupation of Oregon Country, the Hudson's Bay Company was allowed continued use of the fort, which was finally abandoned in 1860.

Named after British Royal Navy Captain George Vancouver, who explored the northwestern Pacific Coast region in the 1790s, Fort Vancouver was originally established on a bluff overlooking the Columbia River in 1824. Rebuilt on the river plain during 1828–29, this post served as the new

Published in 1848, this lithograph based on an original sketch by Lieutenant Henry J. Warre, of the British Army, shows Fort Vancouver from outside the southern stockade wall. (University of Washington Libraries, Special Collections Division)

This lithograph of Fort Nez Perces shows the 20ft-high smooth plank walls topped with a 4ft-high balustrade, which entitled this Hudson's Bay Company fort to be called "the Gibraltar of the Columbia." (*The Fur Hunters of the Far West*, 1855)

Created in 1853 by the artist John Mix Stanley, this lithograph shows the Hudson's Bay Company Fort Walla Walla, located at the confluence of the Columbia and Walla Walla rivers in Washington Territory. Following the destruction by fire of Fort Nez Perces in 1841, this post was built on the same site. The fort itself is in the far middle distance, below the basalt cliffs of the Columbia River Gorge. By 1853 it was protected by adobe-brick walls and had a log-built blockhouse that served as a barbican-style entrance, with two freestanding wooden bastions in opposite corners within the compound. (*Reports of Explorations and Surveys for Pacific Railroad*, 1860)

administrative headquarters and main supply depot of the Hudson's Bay Company in the Columbia District. According to Dr John Scouler, who visited the Columbia River area as medical officer aboard the company brig *William and Ann*, the post was built on "the same plan" as Fort George, but was originally not as large. Fort Vancouver was surrounded by a stockade formed of fir-log pickets, which varied in height depending on the period of construction. Visitors to the post prior to the winter of 1844–45 generally give the height of the stockade as between 20–25ft, although Captain Edward Belcher of the Royal Navy, who visited in August 1839, stated that the pickets were 18ft high, "composed of roughly split pine logs." Those describing the post in 1845 and later give figures that range from 12–20ft, with 15ft as the most frequent estimate. This stockade enclosed an area originally 300ft square, which is believed to have been expanded into a rectangle of about 750 by 450ft by about 1837.

At the northwest corner of Fort Vancouver stood a bastion built during the winter of 1844–45, described by British Lieutenant Merwin Vavasour of the Royal Engineers in March 1846 as a "block house 20 feet square." The two lower stories had loopholes, while an overhanging third level was octagonal and contained eight 3-pdr iron guns. The type of construction employed for the lower walls was known as "French-Canadian," or "posts in the sill," which consisted of a base composed of a sill of heavy timbers, the ends of which were fastened together at the corners by interlocking joints. This sill could rest directly on the ground, but more often it was elevated by wooden blocks or piles. At the corners, and at intervals of 6ft or 10ft along the sill, heavy upright posts were planted by means of mortises. These uprights were grooved, and into the grooves were slid the tenon-shaped ends of horizontally lying logs or timbers, thus filling the empty spaces between the uprights and forming the wall. The three gates providing access to this fort consisted of two in the south (front) wall and one in the north (rear) wall. In the front wall, that to the west was the "main gate" while the easterly one was considered to be the "business gate," through which trading with the Native Americans took place.

As it was established in an area infested with warlike tribes, Fort Nez Perces was built with a double palisade, which was based vaguely on the principle of the medieval concentric castle. Originally constructed in 1818 about 175 miles (280km) inland on the east bank of the Columbia River, this post was described by fur trader Alexander Ross as having palisades that were:

all made of sawn timber. For this purpose wood of large size and cut twenty feet long was sawed into pieces of two and a half feet broad by six inches thick. With these ponderous planks the establishment was surrounded, having on the top a range of balustrades four feet high, which served the double purpose of ramparts and loopholes, and was smooth to prevent the natives scaling the walls. A strong gallery, five feet broad, extended all around. At each angle was placed a large reservoir sufficient to hold 200 gallons of water, as a security against fire, the element we most dreaded in the designs of the natives. Inside of this wall were built ranges of storehouses and dwelling houses for the hands, and in the front of these buildings was another wall, twelve feet high, of sawn timber also, with portholes and slip doors, which divided the buildings from the open square inside. Thus, should the Indians at any time get in, they would see nothing but a wall before them on all sides … and would therefore find themselves in a prison, and infinitely more exposed to danger than if they had been on the outside.

Soon after it was built, Ross claimed it was "the strongest and most complete fort west of the Rocky Mountains, and might be called the Gibraltar of the Columbia." Fort Nez Perces was accidentally burned down in 1841 and rebuilt with stone and adobe the following year, being renamed Fort Walla Walla.

Begun at what became the state capital city of Sacramento in April 1840 by former Swiss army captain Johann Augustus Sutter, Sutter's Fort was at first named Fort New Helvetia (Switzerland), but was occasionally called Fort Sacramento. A visiting scientist in 1843 described the post as having "more the appearance of a citadel than an agricultural establishment." When he reached the main gate of the fort in 1846, Swiss immigrant Heinrich Lienhard observed "the long, black hair and skull of an Indian dangling from one of the gateposts. Even more impressive were the large cannon that stood ominously on either side of the entrance and gave the fort a cold, inhospitable look." After walking 50 or 60ft feet inside the fort he saw "a two-story adobe structure; its door was also guarded by guns, mounted on wheels, that pointed their cold muzzles at all visitors." Measuring 500 by 150ft, Sutter's Fort was also protected by an adobe wall, which was 2½ft thick and 15–18ft high. Because of various land grants, Sutter at first aligned himself with the Mexican authorities and owned more than 150,000 acres of the Central Valley, where he developed vineyards and wheat fields plus vast herds of cattle. Despite it being a flourishing enterprise, Sutter's Fort was abandoned by most of its workers in 1848 with the discovery of gold by carpenter James Marshall at the sawmill Sutter was having built in Coloma, on the American River. All that remained of the post by the 1850s was the central building.

Swiss immigrant Johann Augustus Sutter established Fort New Helvetia, later known as Sutter's Fort, on the site of present-day Sacramento, California, in 1840. This portrait was painted in June 1851 by Stephen William Shaw. (Courtesy of The Bancroft Library)

TYPES OF MILITARY FORT

Adobe-and-stone forts and structures

The Spanish built four presidios along the California coast during the 18th century, all of which were crude-looking affairs in the earliest stages of construction. First built was either a wooden stockade or earthen rampart, followed by structures inside to shelter the people. The latter were made of upright sticks arranged around a square and plastered with mud, with

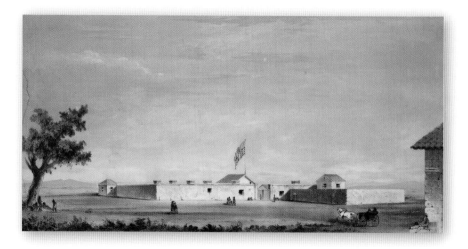

According to Swiss immigrant Heinrich Lienhard, in 1847 Sutter's Fort consisted of a parallelogram about 500ft in length and 150ft in breadth. The main building stood near the center of the compound. A row of shops, storerooms, and barracks lined the walls on all four sides. The principal gates on the east and south were defended by heavy artillery through portholes pierced in the walls. At that time the fort was manned by "about 50 well-disciplined Indians, and 10 or 12 white men, all under the pay of the United States." (Library of Congress, DIG-pga-03551)

dirt floors and flat roofs above covered with leaves, branches, sod, or grass, and plastered down with mud. All four presidios subsequently evolved into forts constructed out of adobe and stone. Constructed under the supervision of Engineer Miguel Costansó, the first was begun at San Diego in 1769. The others were located at Monterey in 1769, San Francisco in 1776, and Santa Barbara in 1782. Although a battery lay close to the shoreline, each presidio was located approximately one mile inland, which placed it safely out of cannonball range of any hostile warship. The basic layout of a presidio was a hollow square protected by high walls with bastions at the corners. A dry moat was dug around the perimeter for added protection. This was usually about 12ft wide and 6ft deep, with excavated soil piled up on the outside lip so attackers would have to climb over it, exposing themselves to defensive fire. The Presidio of San Francisco was originally laid out by Cañizares, pilot of the ship *San Carlos*, in 1776. According to an eyewitness account, he marked out a "square measuring ninety-two vara [roughly 90yds square]

A FORT VANCOUVER, OREGON TERRITORY, *c.*1846

Named after British Royal Navy Captain George Vancouver, who explored the northwestern Pacific Coast region in the 1790s, Fort Vancouver was built in 1829 and served as the administrative headquarters and main supply depot of the Hudson's Bay Company in the Columbia District of what was to become Oregon Territory.

The following structures were enclosed by a 15ft-high stockade measuring approximately 730 by 320ft around the year 1846:

(1) The chief factor's house, also known as the "Big House." Clerks and officers took their meals in a large mess hall, where large parties and dances were also held.
(2) Dwellings.
(3) Indian trade shop. This housed not only the fur-trading operations at the fort, but also the hospital, the doctor's office, and his residence.
(4) Blacksmith shop.
(5) Iron store.
(6) Bakery. It contained two firebrick ovens. As many as four men baked sea biscuits in firebrick ovens for the 200–300 fort employees.
(7) Warehouse.

(8) Harness shop.
(9) Kitchen.
(10) Jail.
(11) Owyhee Church.
(12) Priest's house.
(13) Old Catholic church.
(14) Office 1.
(15) Office 2.
(16) Carpenter shop.
(17) Granary.
(18) Beef store.
(19) Storehouses linked by covered passageway.
(20) Fur storehouses. The multitude of animal pelts, primarily beaver, brought to the fort, were kept here. The furs were cleaned and pressed into bales before being shipped to England.
(21) Powder magazine.
(22) Bastion. Built in 1845 to protect the fort against American threats, this was three stories high with an octagonal upper floor containing eight 3-pdr iron guns.
(23) Flagpole. This flew the ensign of the Hudson's Bay Company with "HBC" in a red field.

each way … with divisions for church, royal offices, warehouses, guardhouse, and houses for soldier settlers."

The defensive walls varied in extent and size. Outer defensive walls were eventually present at Santa Barbara and Monterey. On a tour of inspection in 1777, Governor Felipe de Neve found that Monterey was completely open, and ordered that the situation be rectified with the construction of tall stone walls. The walls of the Presidio de San Carlos de Monterey were about 11ft high and 3ft thick. Those at Santa Barbara varied from 8–12ft. The initial version of this presidio included a temporary wooden stockade about 60yds square, enclosing a number of wooden structures that served as officers' quarters and barracks. Two years later, these began to be replaced by an 80yds square, adobe-walled enclosure with adobe buildings lining the interior walls, all based on stone foundations, with a bastion at the east and west angles. Most of this reconstruction was accomplished in 1784–88.

The Presidio of San Francisco, named in honor of St Francis of Assisi, seems to have lacked a complete set of walls as only three sides were protected. When he visited that post in November 1792, Captain George Vancouver described it as consisting of:

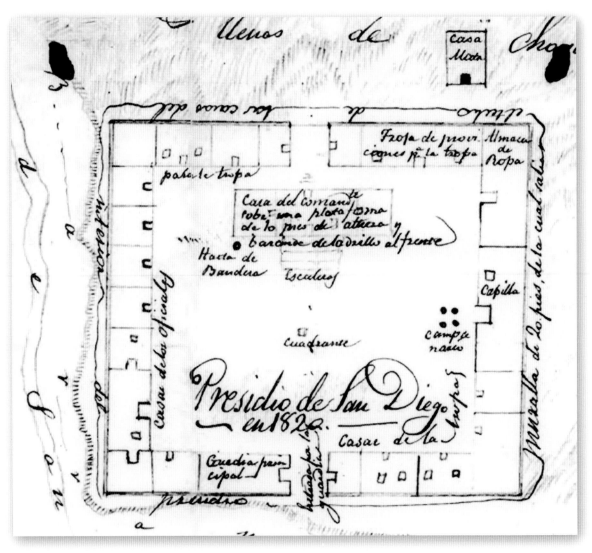

Produced in 1820, this plan of the Presidio of San Diego shows almost all the buildings adjacent to the exterior walls, except for the commander's house. Labelled as *casa de officiales*, the entire north side of the presidio was occupied by the fort officers and their families, non-military personnel, or a combination of the two. (Courtesy of The Bancroft Library)

a square area, whose sides were about two hundred yards in length, enclosed by a mud wall, and resembling a pound for cattle. Above this wall, the thatched roofs of their low small houses, just made their appearance. On entering the Presidio we found one of its sides still unenclosed by the wall, and very indifferently fenced in by a few bushes here and there, fastened to stakes in the ground. The unfinished state of this part, afforded us an opportunity of seeing the strength of the wall, and the manner in which it was constructed. It is about fourteen feet high, and five feet in breadth, and was first formed by uprights and horizontal rafters or large timber, between which dried sods and moistened earth were pressed as close and as hard as possible; after which the whole was cased with earth made into a sort of mud plaster, which gave it the appearance of durability, and of being sufficiently strong to protect them, with the assistance of their firearms, against all the force which the natives of the country might be able to collect.

When he visited the post in the 1850s after its occupation by US troops, American historian Elisha Smith Capron noticed that, at each angle on the outside, was "formally a hollow bastion as high as the main walls, but much thicker, and about fifteen feet square. These were embrasured on two sides for cannon."

Inside the walls of a presidio were the commandant's headquarters (*comandancia*), a barracks building and family quarters, an armory, a chapel, storerooms, a guardhouse, and possibly a corral. At the center lay the parade ground, or *plaza de armas*. At San Francisco and San Diego, the backs of the buildings looked straight out at the dry moat and the countryside beyond, and were all that protected the interior of the presidio. Hence, the garrison was required to fire upon an advancing enemy from the roof or from back windows (if they existed) when under attack. An outer defensive wall was built at Santa Barbara and Monterey, with a row of patios or backyards directly behind, which led to the interior buildings.

Perturbed by the encroachment of the Russians farther north, and the visit of Captain Vancouver aboard HMS *Discovery* in 1792–93, each presidio constructed a *castillo*, or smaller fort, closer to the shoreline, which served as its first line of defense. This contained a cannon emplacement or battery sheltered behind a breastwork or wall made of soil, adobe, or stone. The one at San Diego was known as Castillo de Guijarros (Fort Cobblestones). Established in 1797 on Punta de los Guijarros (Ballast Point) at the entrance to San Diego Bay, it was made of adobe and had two wings mounting ten cannon. At least two of these guns survive. One of them, "El Jupiter," can be seen at Fort Stockton. "El Capitan" is located in Old Town Plaza in San Diego. In use at Monterey from 1792–1822, El Castillo began as an open V-shaped parapet of logs and adobe revetments enclosing a small wooden barracks. Adobe structures were added later. In 1793, Vancouver found its guns mounted on a "sorry kind of barbet battery, consisting of a few logs of wood … cannon, about 11 in number … work cost $450 … was entirely useless." From 1822 to 1846 (the Mexican era) El Castillo was the principal fort protecting the city and harbor of Monterey. Other redoubts in the area included small fortifications at Point Pinos and above El Castillo on Presidio Hill.

Established on what the Spanish called Punta del Cantil Blanco (White Cliff Point), the Castillo de San Joaquin, overlooking the Golden Gate at San Francisco, and the Bateria San Jose, also known as the Bateria de Yerba Buena, on the tip of Point San Jose, were constructed in 1794 and 1797 respectively.

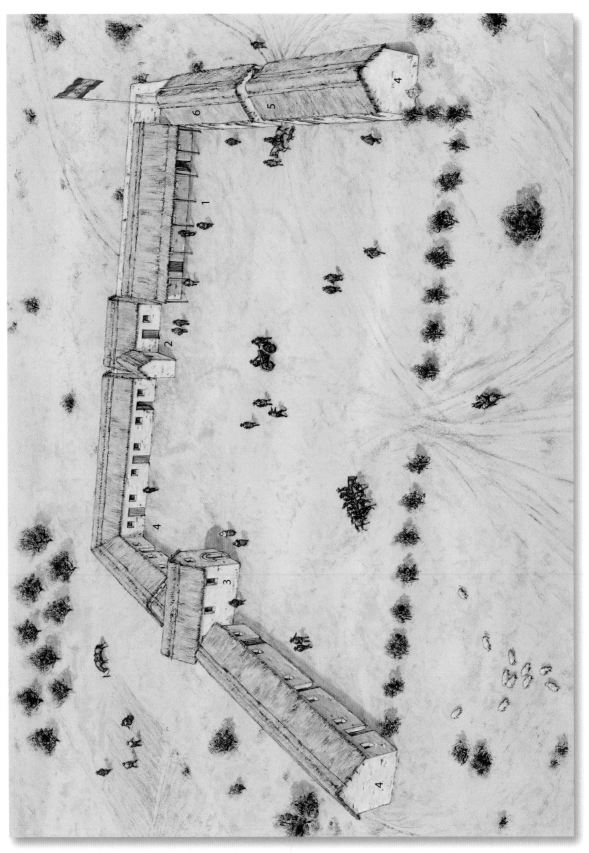

The Castillo de San Joaquin was an irregularly shaped battery composed of 40ft-wide walls topped on the exterior half by merlons. The gun ports measured 2½ft wide at the interior face and flared to 10ft at the exterior. The interior face of the merlons measured 8ft high and sloped toward the exterior to 4ft. Because of the ravages of the climate this fort was in a very sad state of affairs when visited by Pedro de Alberni, Commander of Arms in Alta California, in 1799, as two adobe walls serving as ramparts leading to the blockhouse had been destroyed by storms. Alberni concluded that since "the precipice to the side of the fort is of pure sand, it is possible during one of the earth tremors that are experienced here, it can be split because of its narrowness, thus leaving the aforementioned fortification [cut off from the mainland]." Destroyed by an earthquake in 1815, the earlier fort was replaced by a horseshoe-shaped battery in 1816. At Bateria San Jose five brass 8-pdr cannon were placed in earthworks hastily dug and covered with brushwood fascines. Instead of a permanent garrison, a sentinel visited the installation every day.

The Presidio of San Francisco, around the year 1816. Produced in 1817, this lithograph is based on a drawing by Russian artist Louis Choris, who visited California in 1793. Ohlone men are shown being driven in the direction of a presidio building at the harbor entrance. About 300 Ohlone were used as hard labor to rebuild parts of the fort after Captain Vancouver's visit in 1792. (Courtesy of The Bancroft Library)

Following the independence of Mexico from Spain in 1821, the Presidio of San Francisco received even less attention. Damaged by a minor earthquake in 1827, it was abandoned when the Mexicans relocated to Sonoma in 1835. Falling into American hands as a result of the Bear Flag Revolt of 1836, it was finally occupied by US troops in 1847, and began a long era as headquarters for scattered Army units on the West Coast directing operations to control and protect Native Americans.

When visited by Elisha Capron in the 1850s, the post had been tidied up considerably, as he commented: "The old adobe buildings, and a portion of the walls, are there… The castle of the Mexican commandante and the fort are now occupied by American troops; and neat, whitewashed, picket fences supply the place of a large part of the old walls. The presidio is quadrangular, each side being in length about one hundred yards… The buildings within the enclosure are situated on three sides, extending the whole length of one side [west] and about half the length of the other two [north and south], are of equal height with the walls, and are covered with earthen tile." However, the fort soon fell into a state of disrepair, as post quartermaster R. W. Allen reported in 1855: "I consider all these buildings … of no value and the Post would be improved by their removal. They consist of old Adoba walls dilapidated and moldering down from age with ponderous leaky roofs. In fact they are nothing now but unsightly mud enclosures."

In 1825 a short-lived fortification called the Fuerte de Laguna Chapala was established by the newly formed Mexican Republic in an attempt to reopen an overland route from Sonora to Alta California that had been closed since the Yuma revolt of 1781. Built under the supervision of Junior

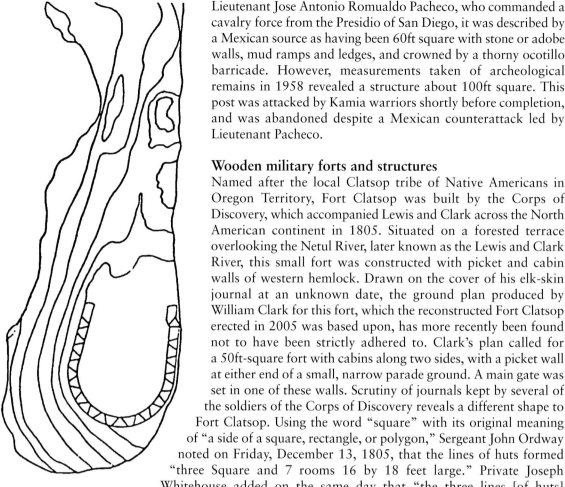

This plan of the Spanish/Mexican fortification Castillo de San Joaquin, drawn by Captain W. H. Warner, US Army, around 1847, shows the horseshoe-shaped battery constructed in 1816. (US National Archives, Cartographic Branch)

Lieutenant Jose Antonio Romualdo Pacheco, who commanded a cavalry force from the Presidio of San Diego, it was described by a Mexican source as having been 60ft square with stone or adobe walls, mud ramps and ledges, and crowned by a thorny ocotillo barricade. However, measurements taken of archeological remains in 1958 revealed a structure about 100ft square. This post was attacked by Kamia warriors shortly before completion, and was abandoned despite a Mexican counterattack led by Lieutenant Pacheco.

Wooden military forts and structures

Named after the local Clatsop tribe of Native Americans in Oregon Territory, Fort Clatsop was built by the Corps of Discovery, which accompanied Lewis and Clark across the North American continent in 1805. Situated on a forested terrace overlooking the Netul River, later known as the Lewis and Clark River, this small fort was constructed with picket and cabin walls of western hemlock. Drawn on the cover of his elk-skin journal at an unknown date, the ground plan produced by William Clark for this fort, which the reconstructed Fort Clatsop erected in 2005 was based upon, has more recently been found not to have been strictly adhered to. Clark's plan called for a 50ft-square fort with cabins along two sides, with a picket wall at either end of a small, narrow parade ground. A main gate was set in one of these walls. Scrutiny of journals kept by several of the soldiers of the Corps of Discovery reveals a different shape to Fort Clatsop. Using the word "square" with its original meaning of "a side of a square, rectangle, or polygon," Sergeant John Ordway noted on Friday, December 13, 1805, that the lines of huts formed "three Square and 7 rooms 16 by 18 feet large." Private Joseph Whitehouse added on the same day that "the three lines [of huts] composed 3 squares, & the other square we intend picketting in, & to have 2 Gates at the two Corners." The next day, the carpenter Patrick Gass provided an even briefer description stating, "We completed the building of our huts, 7 in number." About three months later, as they left the fort for the last time on March 23, 1806, Whitehouse provided one last description of the fort, commenting that it was "built in the form of an oblong Square, & the front of it facing the River, was picketed in, & had a Gate on the North & one on the South side of it."

As all those who mention the fort in their journals agree there were seven rooms and three buildings, there must have been one three-room cabin and two two-room cabins, and these structures encompassed three sides of the enclosed area. In order that the ground plan should not have been lop-sided, the three-room cabin would have been at the back, with the two-room cabins either side. The journal entries of both Meriwether Lewis and the enlisted men agree that the fort had two gates, which would probably have been placed at either end of the picket wall facing the river. Upon Lewis and Clark's departure in 1806, Fort Clatsop decayed rapidly in the wet coastal forests of the Columbia River and nothing remains of the original structure today.

Many military stockade forts built on the West Coast during the remaining pre-Civil War years were similar to the earlier plan adopted by fur-trading companies, which consisted of a picket wall surrounding a square

or rectangular compound with a bastion projecting from at least two corners. In Washington Territory, Fort Henrietta was built by two companies of the First Oregon Mounted Volunteers, commanded by Major Mark A. Chinn, sent to retake the Umatilla Indian Agency and Fort Walla Walla during the uprising generally known as the Yakima War in November 1855. Discovering that the Agency had been burned to the ground and that the Hudson's Bay Company fort was in the possession of "nearly 1,000 Indians" led by Peu-peu-mox-mox, or Yellow Bird, Chinn ordered his men to secure their immediate safety by building a stockade fort near the site of the destroyed Indian Agency. Within three days they had, according to one of the volunteers, constructed "a picket, 100ft square, seven feet high," and had "one block house [or bastion] half built." Consisting of cottonwood, both bastions eventually built at this location had an overhanging second story. This temporary post was subsequently named Fort Henrietta in honor of Henrietta Haller, wife of Major Granville Haller, who provided a wagon to carry provisions to it when no other form of transport was available. Fort Henrietta was abandoned in 1856.

Named after nearby Port Orford, Fort Orford was established in September 1851 on the Oregon coast by a detachment of Co. I, 1st US Artillery, commanded by Lieutenant P. T. Wyman. Initially, 14 buildings were constructed using local cedar logs and lumber, while fixtures and fittings were shipped in from San Francisco. A blockhouse and a stockade wall were erected later during the Rogue River War of 1855–56, following which some of the surrendered Native Americans were held at Fort Orford until they were transported via the steamship *Columbia* to the Grand Ronde Reservation along the coast. The fort was no longer necessary once the hostiles had been removed and it was abandoned in August 1856. Much of this post was dismantled during the following month and the building materials were shipped for use at the second Fort Umpqua, which protected the southern end of the coastal reservation.

Begun in 1856 at the northern end of the Grand Ronde Reservation, most of the wood-frame buildings at Fort Yamhill were later described as being whitewashed in the "cottage" style, with pitched roofs and overhanging eaves. Originally called Camp Hollenbush, Fort Crook was established in the Fall River Valley, California, on July 1, 1857, to protect travelers on the Shasta–Yreka road and the Lockhart Ferries. Built by Co. A, 1st Dragoons, under the command of Captain John W. T. Gardner, it was soon renamed in honor of Lieutenant George Crook, then in command of Co. D, 4th Infantry. This post consisted of about 30 log buildings enclosed within a 12ft-high

Originally a temporary supply camp in Rattlesnake Creek, Oregon Territory, in 1864, Camp Harney was established as a permanent post in 1867, and was named in honor of Brigadier-General William S. Harney. Photographed in 1872, wood-frame and log-built officers' cottages stand at far left, while enlisted men's barracks of unhewn logs are shown at right. Laundresses and married soldiers' quarters are at bottom right nearest the camera. This post served as a supply depot and administrative headquarters until 1880 during the campaign against Northern Paiute bands in Eastern Oregon and the Bannock uprising in the same area. (US National Archives)

Sketched during the Civil War by Private F. Selby, Co. C, 2nd California Cavalry, this bird's-eye view of Fort Crook, in Shasta County, California, shows the log and wood-frame buildings around the parade ground enclosed by a low picket fence. (Courtesy of The Bancroft Library, 1963.002:0227–C)

pine-pole stockade. Crook became a general during the Civil War and gained further fame in the post-Civil War frontier campaigns.

Originally a settler's blockhouse built at Bellingham Bay, in Washington Territory, during 1855, the US Army established a fort at the site in 1856 in response to repeated appeals from the settlers of the area. Protected by a "Stoccade – Built of Red Fir and Cedar, 13 feet high [and] 8 inches thick," enclosing an area measuring 270 by 260ft, and with three gates, Fort Bellingham had bastions of two stories at opposite corners that had loopholes for rifles and embrasures for mountain howitzers. The garrison at this post

C   FORT CLATSOP, OREGON TERRITORY, 1805

Established by the Corps of Discovery, which accompanied the expedition led by Meriwether Lewis and William Clark to find a river route across the American continent, Fort Clatsop was built on a forested terrace overlooking the Netul River in order to provide protection during the winter of 1805. Previously thought to have consisted of two rows of cabins either side of an enclosed area, the latest evidence based on a more accurate interpretation of contemporary diary and journal entries indicates that the fort had cabins occupying most of three sides, with a stockade, or picket wall, projecting towards the riverbank

and forming the fourth side. The building facing the stockade housed the officers' room (**1**), the orderly room (**2**), and quarters for interpreter Toussant Charbonneau and family (**3**). That standing to the left contained a smoke room with an external chimney (**4**) and enlisted men's quarters (**5**), in which a large tree stump served as a table. The third building provided further accommodation for enlisted men (**6**). The main gate and water gate provided access through the stockade to the river, and a sentry box was located by the main gate and outside the smoke room (**7**).

25

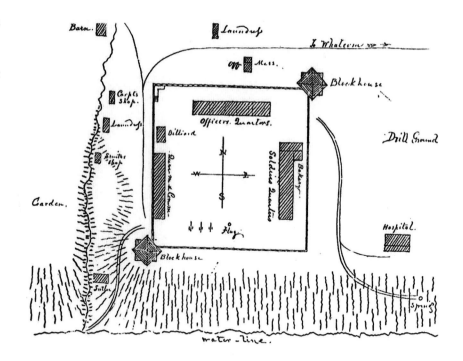

Established in Bellingham Bay, Washington Territory, on August 26, 1856, by Co. D, 9th Infantry, commanded by Captain George E. Pickett, Fort Bellingham was protected by a 13ft-high stockade and had bastions at opposite corners. (US National Archives)

consisted of Co. D, 9th Infantry, commanded by future Civil War Confederate General George E. Pickett, who held the rank of captain in 1855. The chief purpose of this post was to protect the Whatcom coal-mining district from Indian raids and Russian encroachment. In July 1859, Pickett's command was ordered to San Juan Island to oppose British forces in what became known as the Pig War (see below). As a result, they dismantled parts of Fort Bellingham, including one of the blockhouses, and reassembled it on the southern shore of San Juan Island creating Camp Pickett, later called the "Post of San Juan."

Stone-and-brick forts

As a result of the recommendations of the joint Army–Navy Board of 1850, work on a large military installation on Fort Point at the entrance to San Francisco Bay was begun in 1853. This fortification formed part of what became known as the "Third System" of American military architecture, which spanned the period 1850–84, and was so called because it consisted of a third generation of permanent forts built to protect the harbors and coasts of the nation. While nearly 40 similar structures were erected on the Atlantic and Gulf coasts, the fort at Fort Point was the only casemated Third System work built on the Pacific coast. Recommending that it should be "as powerful in its fire on the water as ... the largest of our fortifications on the Atlantic," the Board insisted that the fort built by the Corps of Engineers was to be a massive, multi-storied masonry-and-brick structure. Described in the San Francisco press as "a castle of four tiers of guns, three in casemates, and one, the upper, in *Barbette*," its 5–7ft-thick walls would also provide quarters for officers and enlisted men, storerooms, powder magazines, and sufficient water and provisions to withstand a six-month siege.

Work began in 1853 under the direction of Brevet Major John G. Barnard, with Captain William H. C. Whiting and 2nd Lieutenant Newton F. Alexander in immediate superintendence. Barnard was to become Chief

Engineer under Ulysses S. Grant in 1864, while Whiting planned the new Confederate defenses for Charleston Harbor and Morris Island in 1861. After demolishing the old *castillo* on Fort Point, the construction gang took a year to level the serpentine rock promontory in order to complete a platform measuring 150 by 100yds.

With the foundations completed, work began on the arched casemates that would accommodate the garrison and guns. The floor plan originally chosen for the fort was an irregularly shaped rectangle consisting of four main sides or faces. Three tiers of guns were mounted in the west, north, and east faces, which looked out over the straits of the Golden Gate and across the harbor. Guns were also to be placed on all four faces of the top (barbette) tier. In 1856 two flanking towers, or bastions, were added, which jutted out from the east and west faces. Officially known as the "gorge," the south face contained barracks, powder magazines, and kitchens, plus a small jail. The only entrance to the fort was located at the center of the gorge and consisted of a heavily fortified sally port secured at both ends by heavy oak doors.

Although the first tier of the walls was partially completed using granite, much of the remainder of the structure was built using bricks made to the engineers' specifications in their own brickyard on a hill to the south. Most of the walls had nearly reached completion by late 1859, and the fort was almost ready to receive its armament. Including the two additional bastions, a ten-gun outwork battery, and a detached five-gun counterscarp gallery facing the sally port, "the fort at Fort Point" was able to mount a total of 141 cannon.

By late 1860, Fort Point, which was officially named Fort Winfield Scott in 1882, had still not received its guns, but the outbreak of Civil War in April 1861 prompted Colonel Albert Sydney Johnston, commanding the Department of the Pacific, to order its empty casemates to be manned by Company I, 3rd Artillery, in case of attack by pro-secessionist elements in San Francisco. However, by October of that year 55 guns, including 28 42-pdrs, 11 32-pdrs, and eight 8in. Columbiads, had been mounted inside the fort, mostly on the first tier and the barbette tier. Beginning in 1868,

This Civil War-period view of the interior of Fort Point shows the southern side, which included quarters and office casemates. On the first floor were workshops for the wheelwright, blacksmith, and carpenter. The second floor had officers' quarters, while enlisted men's barracks were on the third floor. A total of 11 32-pdr guns protecting the fort from the landward side can be seen on this part of the fourth tier. (US National Archives)

Fort Point watches over the Golden Gate in 1870 as a three-masted sailing ship plies out into the Pacific Ocean. (Courtesy of The Bancroft Library)

Model 1861 "Rodman" guns, including 10in. smoothbores, were installed in many of its casemates. As with most other Third System forts, Fort Point was never fully armed.

Named La Isla de los Alcatraces (The Island of the Pelicans), Alcatraz Island was first acquired for the US by John C. Fremont, Military Governor of California, in 1846. Two years later, President Millard Fillmore ordered that the Island be set aside specifically for military purposes based upon the acquisition of California from Mexico following the Mexican–American War. From 1853–59 the Corps of Engineers fortified the island under the direction of Major Zebulon B. Tower and the superintendence of Lieutenant Henry Prince.

D FORT POINT, CALIFORNIA, c.1861–65

One of a series of large coastal fortifications that formed part of the "Third System" of American military architecture adopted in the 1820s, which spanned much of the remainder of the 19th century, Fort Point was the only casemated brick-and-stone fortification on the Pacific Coast. Constructed by the US Army Corps of Engineers between 1853 and 1861, it was designed to mount 126 massive cannon and was built in order to prevent the entrance of a hostile fleet into San Francisco Bay. Rushed into completion at the beginning of the Civil War, Fort Point was first garrisoned in February 1861 by Company I, 3rd US Artillery. The fort was occupied throughout the Civil War, but the advent of faster, more powerful rifled cannon made brick forts such as this obsolete. The troops were withdrawn in 1886 and the last cannon were removed around 1900. Parapet wall (**1**); penthouse (**2**); casemates (**3**); lighthouse (**4**); west bastion (**5**); barbette tier (**6**); east bastion (**7**); grass (**8**); embrasures (**9**); quoins (**10**); musket slits (**11**); sally port (**12**); escarp wall (**13**).

Graduating from West Point in 1833, Massachusetts-born John G. Barnard was appointed to the Corps of Engineers and supervised the construction of fortifications during the Mexican War and in Louisiana before being assigned to direct the construction of Fort Point in 1853. He then succeeded Robert E. Lee as superintendent of the US Military Academy from 1855–56, and went on to become Chief Engineer under Ulysses S. Grant in 1864. (Library of Congress, LC-B813-1641 A)

The key element in the fortifications on Alcatraz Island was a number of barbette batteries constructed in the rock with brick-and-stone breastworks. Located mostly around the southwestern side of the island, they commanded the Golden Gate, the inner entrance of which was about 2½ miles from the Alcatraz guns. With steep cliffs around most of its shore, the only access to the island was from a pier on its northeast side commanded by a brick-and-stone casemate containing 11 cannon embrasures. From the pier, the only access to the heights of the island was up a narrow road through a sally port guarded by sentries and three flanking howitzer embrasures. On the slopes near the top were the officers' quarters, the lighthouse, storehouses, and other wood-frame structures. A massive fortified barracks called The Citadel, on the summit, was the most important fortification on the island.

The Citadel was also constructed from brick and stone, which was typical of seacoast fortifications. It was enclosed by a dry moat, or ditch, and its basic plan was more like that of a palisade frontier fort, forming a rectangle with bastions at two diagonal corners. Unusually, this post was designed to be defended solely by rifle fire and did not have a single cannon embrasure. It had three stories, with the first, or basement, level being sunk below ground level. Only this portion of The Citadel survives today. The second story was at ground level, being accessed at each end by a drawbridge across the ditch. The roof provided a third story of protection, being surmounted by a parapet over which the garrison could fire. The basement had musket loopholes all the way around, the second story had narrow windows that could double as musket loopholes, and the third level had slightly wider windows, which also accommodated small-arms fire. The loopholes and windows were all protected by iron shutters, which could be closed against hostile fire.

During the Civil War, Alcatraz became the largest fortress west of the Mississippi River. Although the guns there, and at Fort Point, never fired a shot in anger, they did act as a deterrent to enemy attack on San Francisco Bay. During that conflict the Confederate raider CSS *Shenandoah* attacked the Union commercial whaling fleet in North Pacific waters, and without the deterrent of a strong defense of the Golden Gate that vessel could easily have slipped into the bay to shell San Francisco and perhaps capture gold held in its banks, diverting it to finance the failing Confederacy. After the war, the

importance of Alcatraz as a fort waned as larger and longer-range guns were developed. In 1882 the Citadel was converted into six sets of officers' quarters and served thereafter as an officers' apartment building.

The brick-built Citadel stands in the background of this view of the arsenal and ordnance yard on Alcatraz Island in the late 1860s. Note the absence of cannon embrasures in the walls of this fort, which had rifle loopholes only. (Courtesy of The Bancroft Library)

Parade-ground forts

As on the Great Plains, many of the US military forts established on the West Coast were without the protection of stockade or adobe walls, but consisted of buildings arranged around a parade ground. Indeed, a report from the Surgeon General's Office published in 1870 stated: "The usual plan of our posts is the distribution of the buildings around and fronting on a rectangular plot of ground, used as a parade."

During the 1850s the Presidio of San Francisco began its expansion into a parade-ground fort, with some of its old adobe buildings being replaced by wood-frame structures. A temporary wooden barracks had been erected in 1854 after a storm blew the roof off the old adobe building on New Year's Eve the previous year. A wood-frame hospital was added in 1857. A major transformation occurred in the Civil War years under the supervision of Lieutenant-Colonel R. E. De Russy, commanding the Corps of Engineers, who also directed the placement of defense works in San Francisco harbor. In 1862 a dozen wood-frame "cottages" for officers were constructed along the

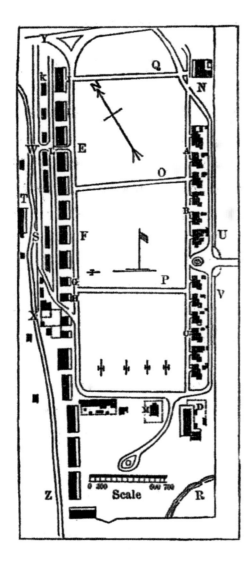

The Presidio in San Francisco, around 1875. The officers' quarters stood to the right of the parade; the enlisted men's barracks to the left; the laundresses' quarters, plus corrals and stables, behind the barracks; and the adobe officers' club at the southern end of the original Spanish Presidio compound. (Author's collection)

eastern side of the Presidio parade ground, which, by 1870, was described as "a parallelogram, 500 by 150 yards." During the same year, seven single-story wood-frame barracks, holding one company each, were built on its west edge, either side of the old 1854 structure. Four others, completed in 1865, measured 120 by 30ft and had two stories, accommodating two companies each. Erected on the west side of the parade during the same year, a new wood-frame two-story guardhouse replaced the old adobe building. A magazine of "rough-hewn stone masonry" was constructed in 1863. Other wood-frame buildings at this post by 1865 included a gun shed and four stables with space for 200 animals, plus a commissary and quartermaster storehouse, all to the northwest of the parade ground. By the end of the Civil War the Presidio of San Francisco had grown from a small collection of adobe and temporary wood-frame structures into a substantial post capable of accommodating over 1,500 officers and men.

On May 13, 1849, two companies of the 1st Artillery arrived aboard the steamer *Massachusetts* at the Hudson's Bay Company trading post Fort Vancouver, in Washington Territory, accompanied by a correspondent for the *Daily National Intelligencer*, of Washington, DC, who reported: "As our officers of the United States Army looked upon this beautiful plain and the fortified appearance of the place their involuntary expression was, 'We hope the Government has bought out the Hudson's Bay Company; what a fine parade ground, and what excellent barracks those storehouses would make for our soldiers. Every thing is exactly fitted for a military post.'" Although the US Government did not buy out the Hudson's Bay Company post at that site until 1860, the Army established a commissary and quartermaster supply base, and subsequently an ordnance depot, called the Columbia Barracks, later known as Fort Columbia and then Fort Vancouver, on a rise 20ft above the Hudson's Bay Company trading settlement. By 1858 this post consisted of a collection of log buildings arranged around a small square parade ground with a blockhouse outside its northeast corner.

Although much of the buildings at Fort Vancouver were destroyed by fire in 1866, they were replaced by a larger post by 1870. Facing the north side of the enlarged parade ground, the officers' quarters consisted of seven log and four wood-frame buildings. According to an 1875 report, the former were built from "carefully-selected logs of red fir" with the gaps "chinked and plastered" with clay, and the interior walls and ceilings lined with "dressed lumber." Double-story wood-frame barracks buildings on opposite ends of the parade ground each had a detached kitchen and mess to the rear. The quarters for married soldiers and laundresses were log huts, "scattered about all parts of the post and greatly out of repair." A two-story wood-frame guardhouse stood facing the south side, with cells on the ground floor and the guardroom above. Other buildings included a hospital (built in 1859), an adjutant's office, bakery, granary, storehouses, and quartermaster's department stables.

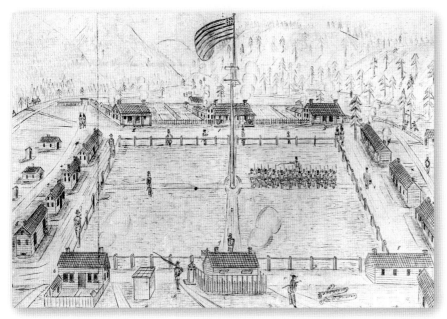

Established on Mill Creek in Washington Territory during 1859, the hewn-log buildings at Fort Colville were arranged on four sides of a square parade, which was enclosed by a rail fence. This drawing, produced in 1867 by an unknown artist, shows infantry drilling and a sentry outside the guardhouse in the center foreground. (University of Washington Libraries, Special Collections Division)

First established in Washington Territory in 1856 near the site of the Hudson's Bay Company's fort of the same name destroyed in 1855, Fort Walla Walla was originally a log cantonment for four companies of the 1st Dragoons and two of the 9th Infantry. In 1858 this post was expanded, with buildings arranged around a rectangular parade ground measuring 325 by 915ft. As at other posts of this type, the officers' quarters and the barracks were situated opposite each other on the longer sides of the parade. The adjutant's office and commissary storehouse occupied one of the shorter sides, with a court-martial room, guardhouse, and post-trader's store at the opposite end. The hospital and quartermaster storehouse were detached, lying to the west and southwest of the parade ground. According to Third Lieutenant Lawrence Kip, of the 3rd Artillery, "the dragoon cantonment" lay about one mile west of the main post. The buildings were described as "all constructed of the same materials and in the same manner, being wood, the outside covered with rough logs placed upright with the cracks battened and the roofs shingled."

Other parade-ground posts in Washington Territory included Fort Colville, established in 1859; Fort Canby (Cape Disappointment), a coastal post begun in 1864; and Fort Townsend, originally constructed in 1856 and re-established in 1874.

One of three parade-ground posts built to monitor the Grand Ronde Reservation in Oregon in the mid-19th century, Fort Hoskins was completed in 1857 with Lieutenant Philip Sheridan in command. Named after Lieutenant Charles Hoskins, who died in the Mexican–American War, this fort was surrounded by a simple low picket fence and sat on a low bluff overlooking a bend in the Luckiamute River. It had an upper and lower parade

Published in *A Report on the Hygiene of the United States Army with Descriptions of Military Posts* in 1875, this plan for Fort Vancouver shows the layout of this parade-ground fort, with the most important buildings arranged around the 400ft-long parade ground. (Author's collection)

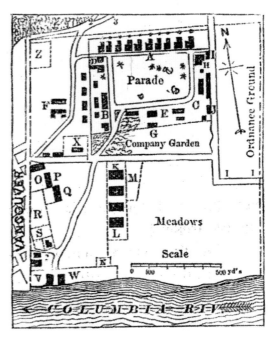

Established as a military post in Washington Territory during 1856, Fort Walla Walla is shown here in 1862, following which it remained a key post during the Civil War, and became an important base of operations during the Modoc, Sheepeater, Nez Perces, and Bannock wars. (University of Washington Libraries, Special Collections Division)

ground, surrounded by about 15 to 20 buildings. The other posts established to police this reservation were forts Yamhill and Umpqua. Among other parade-ground forts in Oregon, Fort Lane was begun in 1853, and named after Brigadier-General Joseph Lane, the first territorial governor of Oregon. During the following year General Mansfield described conditions at this post, stating that, "The quarters of officers, soldiers, hospital and storerooms & c are all of logs erected by the men, and as comfortable as could be expected." Fort Lane was abandoned in 1856.

One of the earliest military posts in northern California, Fort Reading was named after Major Pierson B. Reading, paymaster of the California Volunteers during the Mexican–American War and pioneer settler in California. Situated by Cow Creek, this two-company fort was begun in 1852 and was primarily intended to protect the mining district from Native American "depredations." Often flooded during the rainy season, its main buildings consisted of adobe arranged around a small parade ground, with log and wood-frame structures spread south along the riverbank. A member of the US Surveying Expedition arriving there in July 1855 described it as "the most unhealthy portion of the United States' possessions." Although the garrison was withdrawn in 1856, the post was intermittently occupied until 1867, when it was finally abandoned.

Established at Suisun Bay, California, in 1849, the military complex at Benicia consisted of ordnance-and-supply depots and a parade-ground post. Standing on the west side of the parade, the enlisted men's barracks consisted of a wood-frame building that had been constructed in Maine and shipped in kit form, and at "great expense, all the way around Cape Horn." According to a report in the *Daily National Intelligencer*, of Washington, DC, when this building accidentally burned down in July, 1853, it was "two stories high, neatly painted, with double balconies in front and rear, and ... lofty windows ... shaded by green Venetian blinds." Abandoned in 1866, the Benicia Barracks was re-established later the same year and became headquarters for the 1st Cavalry and a receiving depot for cavalry recruits.

THE PRINCIPAL ELEMENTS OF DEFENSE

Blockhouses and bastions

Wooden blockhouses were common on the West Coast. Those built by the Russians in Alaska and farther south were usually octagonal or heptagonal two-story structures. Established on Castle Hill at Sitka in 1803, those at Fort Archangel Gabriel were eight-sided with two tiers of cannon. When US naval forces under Commodore John Drake Sloat, commander of the Pacific Squadron, landed at Monterey Bay, California, in July 1846, they built a new fortification, which included a log blockhouse, on Presidio Hill above El Castillo, the old Spanish fort.

Uprisings among the Native Americans of the Northwest during the winter of 1855–56 caused the military to construct blockhouses at numerous strategic points. Farmers and settlers also banded together to build them for the protection of their families and property. Most of these followed the pattern found on the Central and Northern Plains, being two stories high with the upper story overhanging the ground floor. The upper story was either parallel to the ground floor, or was turned at an angle of 45 degrees to it, eliminating any blind spots on the corners and allowing for a 360-degree field of fire. Incorporating about six musket loopholes per side on each floor, they were usually not built to accommodate cannon.

Standing at the entrance to the Grand Ronde Valley in Oregon, and built in 1856, the blockhouse at Fort Yamhill was 20ft square with a hipped roof above its diagonally-set second story and smaller roof sections covering the protruding part of the ground floor. This fort also included officers' quarters, barracks, a hospital, a carpenter shop, and laundress quarters, built at first under Lieutenant William Hazen and subsequently under the direction of Lieutenant Philip Sheridan, both of whom became Civil War generals. Built after the same pattern, and originally called the Yaquina Bay Blockhouse, the Siletz Blockhouse was begun in late August 1856. After the Siletz Indian Agency was established, the Army dismantled and moved the blockhouse six miles in September 1857. The last contingent left there on June 23, 1866, bound for Fort Yamhill.

In the Puget Sound area of Washington Territory, volunteers and Army troops built at least 33 blockhouses during the period generally known as the Yakima War. Consisting of hand-hewn logs, the Alexander Blockhouse

Named after Camp Barbour, the single-story Barbour Blockhouse was the scene in 1851 of treaty negotiations between a three-man commission, which included George W. Barbour, and the Mariposa people, who were then in a state of armed rebellion. In a dilapidated condition when photographed in 1914, the loopholes are still visible in the walls. The larger openings were embrasures for cannon. (Library of Congress, HABS CAL, 10-MILL.V,1)

The Crockett Blockhouse was erected on the John Crockett farm, Whidbey Island, Washington Territory, during the Native American uprisings in the 1850s. (University of Washington Libraries, Special Collections Division)

constructed by settler John Alexander on Whidbey Island had its upper story overhanging the ground floor in parallel fashion. This structure was also enclosed by a 10ft-high stockade, which those on the second floor of the blockhouse could see over. The stockade walls were notched every few feet so that riflemen could fire on attackers. Broken glass and jagged metal fragments were embedded in the top of the stockade as added deterrents to climbing. Also on Whidbey Island, the Jacob Ebey Blockhouse was one of

In late 1855 the citizens of Seattle, with help from the crew of the Navy sloop of war *Decatur*, built a blockhouse on the knoll that was then still at the waterfront foot of Cherry Street. The sloop's physician, John Y. Taylor, drew the earliest rendering of the log construction, which is shown here. (Courtesy, Yale University, Beinecke Library)

four built in 1855 near Coupeville by Jacob Ebey, father of Colonel Isaac N. Ebey, whose later death by the hands of Haida Indians was responsible for the construction of some of the island's further defenses. A 12ft-high palisade originally surrounded Ebey's dwelling and connected four blockhouses, one at each corner. Two of these structures remain today.

What Professor Dennis Hart Mahan, of West Point, termed an "American Blockhouse," was built with the assistance of sailors and marines of the USS *Decatur* prior to the Native American attack on Seattle in January 1856. A barn-like structure with a pitched roof and an outer layer of horizontal logs, the North Blockhouse unusually had small upper-story bastions containing musket loopholes overhanging at roof height from its northeast and southwest corners. According to a sketch produced by surgeon John Y. Taylor from the deck of the *Decatur*, this structure also had horizontal loopholes along its side and several vertical ones cut into its gable ends.

By the end of March 1856, Colonel Silas Casey, 9th Infantry, who had arrived in Puget Sound at the beginning of the year to take command of Fort Steilacoom, had established Fort Slaughter, which consisted of a blockhouse, storehouses, and a hospital on Muckleshoot Prairie, about 25 miles south of Seattle. During this same period, a detachment led by Captain Erasmus D. Keyes, 3rd Artillery, destroyed a small fortification built by the Native Americans on Porter's Prairie, which was described as "20 by 40 feet, built of large logs."

Regarding log blockhouses in California, the first permanent settler in the Napa Valley, thanks to a Mexican land grant, was George C. Yount, who built

Built in the American style, the British blockhouse at what became known as English Camp on San Juan Island was erected during the Pig War of 1859. (University of Washington Libraries, Special Collections Division)

a two-story wooden blockhouse in 1836, which was replaced the following year by an adobe structure about 100ft in length pierced with loopholes. The blockhouse built at Camp Barbour, close to the later site of Fort Miller, in the San Joaquin Valley, was established in 1850 to protect miners from marauding Mariposa, who were then in a state of armed rebellion. A single-story building constructed from horizontal rough-hewn logs by members of the Mariposa Battalion, it had a pitched, lean-to shingle roof with small loopholes for muskets and large gun ports to accommodate cannon. On April 29, 1851, a three-man commission including George W. Barbour negotiated a treaty with the Mariposa people at this blockhouse.

The bloodless Pig War of 1859 was sparked off when an American settler shot a pig owned by a Hudson's Bay Company employee, but was caused in the longer term by a dispute over where the boundary lay between the US and Canada. This conflict resulted in British forces placing a blockhouse on the northwest coast of San Juan Island in Washington Territory. In response, US troops initially commanded by Captain George E. Pickett threw up a substantial earthwork on a hill near the southern tip of the island in order to allow them to defend against ships coming to the island from Victoria. A two-story structure built in the American style, the British blockhouse at what became known as English Camp was brought from the British Fort on Vancouver Island. It had its upper story turned at an angle of 45 degrees from the lower one, with a single gun port facing out across

Photographed when the British North American Boundary Commission survey crews arrived in May 1860, the blockhouse with an octagonal-shaped third story built by the Hudson's Bay Company in 1845–46 is seen behind tents in the northwest corner of Fort Vancouver. A belfry of the type erected in the 1850s stands in the foreground. (Library of Congress, LC-USZC4-11409)

E **CUTAWAY SHOWING THE CONSTRUCTION AND INTERIOR OF THE FORT BORST BLOCKHOUSE, WASHINGTON TERRITORY, 1855**

The Fort Borst Blockhouse was built in 1855 near the junction of Chehalis and Skookumchuct rivers by Captain Francis Goff and five soldiers of the Oregon Volunteers, or militia, as a grain-storage depot during the wars with the Native Americans. It was a strategic point on the military road between forts

Vancouver and Steilacoom. The blockhouse at this post was designed with loopholes in the walls of the upper story and the floor of the overhang. This wintry scene shows volunteers loading grain sacks onto an ox-driven farm cart, while a sentry keeps lookout above.

Garrison Bay and loopholes on all four sides. Notches cut in its lower-story walls could be knocked out in order to produce further loopholes if needed. It had a single-story lean-to roof projecting out from the landward side to protect the ground-floor entrance, and was painted white, as were other buildings at the post. Garrisoned by Royal Marines from 1860–72, a shot was never fired in anger from the English Camp blockhouse, it being used largely as a guardhouse. When the present international boundary was finally fixed in 1873, San Juan Island was reputedly the last place in the US where the British standard was officially displayed.

Earthworks, ditches, and moats

Begun during the Mexican–American War when the naval forces of Commodore John Drake Sloat, commander of the Pacific Squadron, landed at Monterey Bay in July 1846, the earthen redoubt at Fort Mervine was set out in the form of a redan (an arrow-shaped salient angle) with auxiliary flanks. Behind this stood various log structures including a blockhouse, a barracks (measuring 100 by 17ft), a six-room two-story officers' quarters, plus a stone magazine and storehouse measuring 75 by 25ft.

An earthen redoubt was built by US troops under Lieutenant-Colonel Silas Casey, 9th Infantry, near Camp Pickett, also known as American Camp, on the southern end of San Juan Island at the start of the Pig War of 1859–72. This fortification was later nicknamed "Robert's Gopher Hole," as its construction was supervised by 2nd Lieutenant Henry Martin Robert, Corps of Engineers, who had graduated from West Point in 1857. According to the diary of William A. Peck, Jr., a soldier under Robert's command, the fort was "laid out of an irregular form 425 feet long above the natural ground; ditch 20 feet wide, not less than 8 feet deep." A further diary entry from Peck indicated that the earthwork had been altered two days later but gave no new dimensions. When the historian Hubert Howe Bancroft measured the site in 1887, he noted essentially the same dimensions as today (i.e. 350ft on the west side, 100ft on the southeast, and 150ft on the northeast). Guns taken from the USS *Massachusetts*, which served as headquarters for Lieutenant-General Winfield Scott, who had arrived to negotiate with the British, were used to fortify the post, and five gun

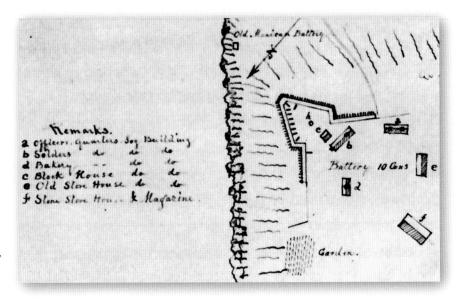

Established at Monterey, California, in July 1846 during the Mexican–American War following the landing of US naval forces commanded by Commodore John Drake Sloat, the earthen redoubt at Fort Mervine guarded the sea approaches and protected various log structures behind it, which included a blockhouse. (Mansfield Report, 1853–54)

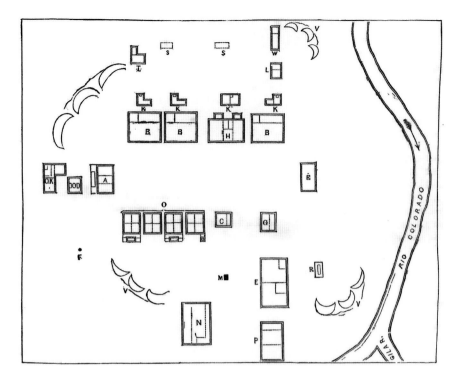

The earthen bastions thrown up in 1861 are shown in this ground plan of Fort Yuma, in southern California, which was included in the *Report on the Hygiene of the United States Army* published in 1875. (Author's collection)

platforms were completed, two of which were at the corners. The parapet stood 7ft above the interior, with an exterior ditch varying from 18–33ft in depth, the bottom of which was 3–5ft across.

In July 1863 the name of this post was changed to Camp San Juan, and it remained so until March 1867 when it was called Camp Steele, after General Frederick Steele, who commanded the Department of the Columbia at that time. It was soon afterwards changed to Camp San Juan Island, on account of there being a post in Wyoming Territory called Fort Fred Steele (see Fortress 28: *Forts of the American Frontier 1820–91, Central and Northern Plains*). The guns in its redoubt never fired a shot in anger. In fact, only three were ever emplaced and these merely fired a salute to General Scott when he visited Griffin Bay on November 7, 1859. Scott had ordered work on the fortress stopped after he and British Columbia Governor James Douglas agreed to reduce their forces on the island.

Following over a decade of confrontation and military bluster, during which time the local British authorities consistently lobbied London to seize back the Puget Sound region entirely whilst the US was busy elsewhere with the Civil War, in 1871 Great Britain and the US signed the Treaty of Washington. This dealt with various differences between the two nations, including border issues with the newly formed Dominion of Canada. Among the results of the treaty was the decision to resolve the San Juan dispute by international arbitration, with Kaiser Wilhelm I of Germany chosen to act as arbitrator. The German ruler referred the issue to a three-man arbitration commission, which met in Geneva, Switzerland, for nearly a year. On October 21, 1872, the commission decided in favor of the United States, following which the military forces of both nations withdrew from the island.

Built by troops commanded by Captain Samuel P. Heintzelman, 2nd Infantry, on the north bank of the Colorado River in 1850 to protect the

This drawing shows Fort Yuma during the 1850s. Distinguished by crenellations on its adobe upper floor and lookout tower or bastion, the commanding officer's quarters stands at the end of the small parade ground. (California State Military Museum)

emigrants of Southern California from the attacks of hostile Native Americans, Fort Yuma was based around a parade ground to which earthworks were added by the 1st California Volunteer Infantry in 1861 to counter the threat of Confederate attack. On November 13 of that year Lieutenant-Colonel Joseph R. West, the officer responsible for their construction, reported to Colonel James H. Carleton, commanding the Southern District of California, "I am throwing up one work 350ft – faces on a low hill west of and adjoining the fort – and three smaller ones at different points. This gives us plenty of work. Also drilling all spare time, and artillery detachment at it constantly." By 1875 these earthworks were described in

Published in the *Illustrated London News* on May 24, 1873, Lake Tule is seen in the background of this engraving showing Camp Van Bremer, which served as the headquarters for operations against the Modoc in the Lava Beds on the California–Oregon border. Note the earthwork redoubt at center left and the tents set out around a parade ground at center right. An Army signal station can be seen in the foreground. (Author's collection)

Army Inspection Report 561 as being "unpretentious intrenchments scattered along the slopes of the bluff, which command the river and the bottom-lands adjacent. They are not visible from the river and the visitor is not aware of their existence until he steps to the edge of the bluff and looks down upon their gabion revetments. They were constructed for barbette guns, but are now dismantled."

Named after slain Civil War general and former Washington Territory governor, Isaac Stevens, Fort Stevens was established at the mouth of the Columbia River in 1863 to guard against potential British attack during ongoing regional tensions related to the Pig War. It was initially referred to as the "Fort at Point Adams," and was the primary military installation in the three-fort Harbor Defense System, the other two forts in the system being Cape Disappointment (Fort Canby) and Fort Columbia on the Washington side of the river. The post and works at Fort Stevens were built under the supervision of US engineers, and were first occupied by a company of the 8th California Volunteers on April 25, 1865. Mounting 34 guns, it was described in the *Army and Navy Journal* in May 1867 as being "constructed of earth, is rectangular oblong in shape, with bastions at the angles; a wide and deep wet moat surrounds the entire work; the magazine, ball and bomb-proof, is within the enclosure." Standing in the rear of the earthworks, wood-frame buildings formed "a hollow square" around a parade ground.

LIFE IN THE FORTS

Trade forts

Daily life in a trade fort varied according to the location and ownership of the post. Those managed by the Hudson's Bay Company were usually well run. Bells were rung at certain times during the day. When he visited Fort Vancouver in 1841, Lieutenant Charles Wilkes, of the US Exploring Expedition, observed that the bell was rung "at early dawn" to call the men to work. It sounded again at eight for breakfast, at one for dinner, and at six

This drawing of fur trading at Fort Nez Perces (also known as Fort Walla Walla) was drawn by Joseph Drayton, one of several artists hired for a US naval expedition led by Lieutenant Charles Wilkes from 1838–42, and depicts chief trader Archibald McKinley inspecting pelts offered by a group of Native Americans. (Oregon Historical Society Research Library, OrHi 964)

The inscription on this replica of the original bell used at Fort Ross translates as: "Cast in the St Petersburg Foundry of Master Craftsman Mikhail Makharovich Stukolkin." Based on a rubbing made from the original, the bell was recast using the same materials as the original. (Fort Ross State Historic Park)

when labor ceased for the day. On Saturdays the peal that marked the end of work came at five in the afternoon in order to provide time for the servants to collect their weekly rations. On Sundays the bell called the fort's population to worship. It likewise tolled for deaths, weddings, fires, and various other occasions.

When the Native Americans arrived to trade, they were generally prevented from entering the interior of the fort. At some posts, such as Fort Nez Perces, they were permitted to negotiate only through an aperture in the outside picket wall. Elsewhere they were allowed past the first gate and into an area known as the "Indian Hall," a trading shop where business took place. There the process of bartering was encouraged by the issuing of liquor in order to "regale" or welcome the visitors.

The elements took their toll on the occupants of trade forts. The weight of snow could collapse buildings, and gale-force winds could damage stockade walls and bastions. Although the dwellings inside Fort Nez Perces were stoutly built, with wooden walls about 6in. thick, their roofs were prone to leakage when it rained as the pitch on their split cedar roofs was too low, allowing water to seep through the straw-and-mud covering.

During mealtimes in a trade fort, separate tables were laid for officers and laborers. At certain factories the latter drew rations from the steward, as in the military. The sole and ultimate object of all was to make money, and all were busy. However, when an isolated post manager was caught with no winter occupation to hand, time dragged wearily by. According to Gray, such periods were usually "a rather tame existence ... passed in a bleak and dreary wilderness, the howl of the coyote and warning rataplan of the rattlesnake the only bucolic music; wild beasts and savages the only adjacent neighbours."

Military posts

The presidios of California were built by the soldiers themselves with the help of Native American labor. Evidence that Native Americans also participated in their construction was found at Monterey, where the expense sheets submitted to the paymaster general in Mexico included sums paid to the indigenous population for help in building the chapel. At Santa Barbara, José Francisco Ortega reported that some of the Chumash people eagerly worked for beads, and stated that if only he had more beads the work would have progressed even faster. At Santa Barbara, sailors from the Spanish frigate *Santiago*, commanded by Captain Esteban Martinez, were pressed into service. Of special value to construction crews were the skilled craftsmen who had received training at San Blas, the primary West Coast port for trade between Mexico and Alta California, and who had contracted for service in California. Native American workers and their families became a permanent feature of life at a presidio, and may have preferred living there rather than at a mission, where life was more regimented. To some Spanish officials, their presence was welcome as it contributed much to the process of conquest in California.

The adobe structure of many presidio walls and buildings was not conducive to longevity. After several seasons of rain in northern California, walls often collapsed and had to be rebuilt, as at San Francisco in 1779. Winter in a presidio was very uncomfortable, as rivulets of mud washed through skimpy thatched roofs and dropped onto the heads of the garrison. Under their feet, dirt floors turned to mud in persistent rain or to dust in summer. Even with a more weathertight roof covered with natural asphaltum, which was abundant in southern California, it often melted and dropped in globules onto the occupants, their furnishings, and the floor.

In contrast, life was much improved for the soldiers of the US Army who garrisoned the Presidio of San Francisco by 1865. Inspecting the commodious accommodation for the enlisted men in February of that year, General Irwin McDowell reported: "Each company has a large room by itself, about 60 feet long by 20 in width. About the sides of the room bunks are erected, three in a tier. The room is heated with a large stove in the centre, and seats and tables are placed in each room for the convenience and comfort of the men. In addition to the bunk room they have a dining or mess room, connected with which is a company kitchen." Life was less comfortable at Fort Point, as the interior courtyard was surrounded by 45ft-high walls that enveloped the garrison in deep shadow, making the living quarters for enlisted men dark and dank. The only heat provided came from small fireplaces in each of the third-tier gorge casemate rooms. The men slept in two-tier bunks with 12 bunks to a casemate and 24 men to a smoke-filled room already heavy with the odour of stale tobacco and unwashed and wet woolen uniforms. Officers were accommodated with greater comfort on the second tier of the gorge. Assigned individual bedrooms, they were allowed personal furnishings such as curtains and carpets. A few married officers were permitted to bring their wives into the post, and before the end of the Civil War several frame buildings were erected south of the fort to serve as married quarters.

Possibly photographed by a British naval officer from the HMS *Satellite*, Battery D, 3rd Artillery, poses with a 6-pdr gun at the American Camp Pickett, on San Juan Island, during the Pig War of 1859. According to a correspondent for the *Alta California*, who visited the post at the same time, the US garrison was "wholly dressed in new uniforms." (US National Park Service)

Discipline and daily routine was strict at Fort Point and the Presidio, as it was at most of the larger US military posts on the West Coast. Describing Army life at Camp Pickett, on San Juan Island, at the beginning of the Pig War in October 1859, a correspondent of the *Alta California*, of San Francisco, wrote:

> The reveille is beaten at 5½ o'clock – and the fifes, drums and trumpets, keep up a general hub-bub for nigh an hour. The men breakfast, but the major portion of the officers content themselves with a cup of hot coffee and a slice of toast. At eight o'clock there is a general battalion drill. The martial music sounds, and each company, with its officer, or officers, comes upon the ground in double quick time... Drill over, the men divest themselves of their new uniforms, and repair to their various labors... Dinner is ready at 12½ o'clock; previous to which the detachments at work on the redoubt are relieved; and after the meal fresh hands take their place. At 3½ o'clock the recall is sounded; at 4 o'clock the whole force is paraded, and the orders of the day announced. At 5 o'clock the officers mess. Night soon closes in, and the tattoo beats at 8 o'clock. Such is the routine of a soldier's life.

Day-to-day life in smaller and more remote military posts was less exciting, and consisted primarily of mundane chores. At Fort Hoskins, in Oregon Territory, a lack of meaningful activity and lax discipline resulted in low morale, and desertion was commonplace. The higher command frowned on soldiers fraternizing with the local Native Americans. Lieutenant H. H. Garber faced a court martial over an incident involving a Native American woman he took on a trip to Fort Vancouver. Garber was suspended from rank and pay for six months in 1858 and subsequently died in the fort hospital in October 1859.

After enlisting for active service during the Civil War, many Californian, Oregonian, and Washingtonian state volunteers instead spent much of their time waiting for something to happen. While they were far from the battlefields back east, their battles at isolated posts such as Fort Reading, in northern California, were no less real as they fought hunger, rain, snow, monotony, and isolation. Posted to Fort Hoskins in 1865, Private William M. Hilleary recorded in his diary: "It required about two cords [a stack of wood 4 by 8 by 8ft] every day to keep up the fires in the fort. We had no stoves, not even cook-stoves, but open fires in every room... The mud is so deep that six mules haul only one quarter of a cord at a load... Rain and Snow, disagreeable under foot... Stormy all day... Snow, Rain, Mud, Water!!!"

Based at one of the hottest locations near the West Coast, the garrison at Fort Yuma, in southern California, had the opposite experience, with an average temperature of 105 degrees Fahrenheit (40 degrees Celcius) in the shade from April through June each year, and no rainfall. When he visited, traveler John Martin Hammond wrote:

> Being so excessively dry the air at this post plays strange pranks with articles made for use in less arid climate, as many a young officer's wife has found to her cost when bringing trunks and other household paraphernalia to her new home. Furniture put together in the North and brought here falls to pieces... Ink dries so rapidly upon the pen that it requires washing off every few minutes... Newspapers required to be unfolded with care, for if handled roughly they crumble. Boxes of soap that weigh twelve pounds when shipped

to Fort Yuma weigh only ten pounds after having been there for several weeks… The effort to cool one's self with an ordinary fan is vain, because the surrounding atmosphere is of higher temperature than the body. The earth under foot is dry and powdery and hot as flour just ground, while the rocks are so hot that the hands cannot be borne upon them.

The upper story of the barracks building at Fort Townsend, on Port Townsend Bay, Washington Territory, was heated by two stoves by 1885. Also note the gun-racks and kit arranged above each metal-frame bed. (University of Washington Libraries, Special Collections Division)

THE FORTS AT WAR

Alaska

The Russians experienced native hostility in Alaska during May 1802 when the Tlingit people and their allies, who had been supplied with "guns, ammunition, and spirits" by British and American traders, attacked Fort Archangel Gabriel in Sitka Bay, Alaska, while most of the garrison was out hunting. All of the officers and 30 men were killed, and the warehouses and cattle sheds, plus vessels lying at anchor off the settlement, were set on fire and destroyed. During the spring of 1804 a force consisting of about 1,000 Russians and Aleuts commanded by Alexander Baranov sailed in a flotilla of four vessels from Kodiak to retake Fort Archangel Gabriel. On arrival, Baranov found the Native Americans occupying a log fort protected by a breastwork "two logs thick," on a bluff called Katlean's Rock, or the Kekoor, at the mouth of the Indian River. The Russians landed and attempted to storm this fort but were repulsed with 26 killed or wounded, Baranov being included among the latter. Following a further attack the next day led by Captain Lisiansky of the ship *Neva*, the Tlingit defenders promised to surrender and offered hostages. When they failed to keep their word, the Russians brought up some of the ship's guns mounted on a raft and opened fire. The Native Americans endured the ferocious bombardment until nightfall, when they abandoned the fort after strangling their infant children and killing their dogs, so that no sound might reveal their escape. The Russians then built another fort, called New Archangel, which consisted of a stockade with a blockhouse at each corner, protecting three substantial buildings.

Alta California

The Spanish fortifications at Monterey and Santa Barbara came under attack when two corsair ships commanded by Hipólito de Bouchard, a French-Argentine adventurer, sailed along the California coast in 1819. Flying the flag of Argentina, then the United Provinces of the Rio de la Plata, Bouchard had already attacked the Spanish colonies of Chile and Peru whilst under the command of the Argentine-Irish Admiral William Brown. He was also the first Argentine to circumnavigate the world, during which he blockaded the Spanish-owned port of Manila, and in Hawaii recovered an Argentine privateer that had been seized by mutineers. On November 20, 1819, he sailed into Monterey Bay aboard the frigate *La Argentina*, which was accompanied by the corvette *Santa Rosa*. Warned of his approach, Pablo Vicente de Solá, the last Spanish governor of Alta California, ordered the removal of two-thirds of the gunpowder stocked in the military outposts, and advised that all the valuables in the city should be withdrawn.

After approaching the coastline, Bouchard discovered that the draft of his larger frigate was too deep for the shallow waters of the bay and had her towed out of the range of the Spanish guns using small boats. Once she was out of range, Bouchard ordered Captain Sheppard, commanding the corvette, with its lighter draft, to land a party of 200 men armed with muskets and pikes under cover of darkness. As his men were exhausted from towing *La Argentina*, Sheppard decided to wait until dawn before launching the attack, only to discover that he had anchored too close to the shore and was in range of the Spanish guns, which opened fire, forcing him to surrender. Most of the crew and landing party, which included Hawaiian mercenaries, were either killed or swam ashore to face capture, although some were rescued by small boats sent from *La Argentina*. Four days later, Bouchard effected a landing in a creek about three miles from Monterey and, after an hour-long attack, finally captured the shore battery and the presidio. The Argentine corsairs occupied Monterey for six days, during which time they stole cattle, destroyed the fortifications, and burned the artillery headquarters and the governor's residence.

Chief Manager of the Russian–American Company and first governor of Russian Alaska, Alexander Baranov was wounded leading an attack on a Native American blockhouse in Sitka Bay in 1804. He wears the gold medal of the Order of Saint Vladimir around his neck, which had been awarded by Tsar Alexander I the previous year. (*Overland Monthly*)

Early frontier wars

As European traders and armed forces established forts on the West Coast, so they came under attack or were involved in campaigns against the Native Americans. In May 1849, a "large body" of Suquamish braves arrived outside Fort Nisqually, a subsidiary trading post of the Hudson's Bay Company on Puget Sound in Oregon Territory, intent on attacking friendly Native Americans in the immediate vicinity. Although the post manager tried to calm the situation, the Suquamish attempted to force their way through the gate of the fort. During the brutal struggle that ensued, one defender was killed and two were wounded. The young son of a friendly Native American was also mortally wounded. Following an investigation later that year conducted by Governor Joseph Lane, and a reward offered of "eighty blankets," the perpetrators were apprehended, tried, and executed.

During August 1849, Captain Bennett H. Hill, 1st Artillery, arrived in the area to establish Fort Steilacoom on the southern extremity of Puget Sound. This post served as a supply depot and refuge from 1849–68 and as headquarters for the 9th Infantry during the Yakima War of 1855–56. During that conflict, prominent Puget Sound pioneer Ezra Meeker sought shelter with his family at the post, following which he recalled the scene as a "sorry mess … women and children crying, cows bellowing, sheep bleating, dogs howling … utmost disorder."

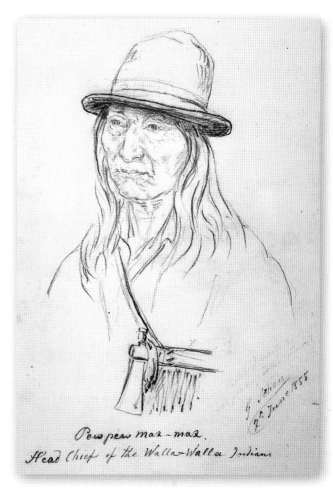

Peu pew max - max.
Head Chief of the Walla-Walla Indians

Warriors led by Walla Walla Chief Peu-peu-mox-mox, or Yellow Bird, captured Fort Walla Walla in November 1855. This sketch was made on June 7, 1855, by soldier-artist Gustav Sohon. (Washington State Historical Society)

Regarding fighting during the Yakima War, the Hudson's Bay Company Fort Walla Walla and nearby Umatilla Indian Agency were overrun and captured by about 1,000 warriors led by Peu-peu-mox-mox, or Yellow Bird, during November 1855. A relief force composed of two companies of Oregon Mounted Volunteers, commanded by Major Mark Chinn, set out from The Dalles, on the Columbia River, on November 15, and five days later were within striking distance of the stricken fort. While waiting to be joined by a force led by Lieutenant-Colonel James Kelly, they built Fort Henrietta, a small stockade post, from which one of the volunteers wrote: "We are anxiously awaiting the arrival of reinforcements and field pieces, for old Peu-peu-mox-mox has been feasting on the 'good things' in Walla Walla long enough; we want to have a chance to 'pitch in.' The old fellow says he is going to 'winter in Walla Walla;' we hope to winter him in warmer regions."

Once united, the Oregonians advanced on Fort Walla Walla to find the log-and-adobe structure abandoned and largely destroyed. However, they pursued the Native Americans in a running battle lasting several days. On December 5, 1855, Peu-peu-mox-mox and five other braves approached Kelly for a parley. Believing it to be a trap, Kelly took them as hostages, and all six warriors were killed while "attempting to escape" during the fighting

two days later. Following this, Kelly's command withdrew closer to the ruined Indian Agency where they established "a permanent camp for the winter," which they named Fort Bennett, in honor of Captain Bennett, commander of Co. F, Oregon Mounted Volunteers, who rested "beneath its stockade."

In January 1856 Native Americans attempted to attack Seattle, in Washington Territory. Warned by Si'ahl, chief of the friendly Duwamish people, the inhabitants of this small coastal community prepared their defenses by converting two buildings into blockhouses with the help of seamen from the USS *Decatur*, commanded by Commander Guert Gansevoort, which had been assigned to patrol the local waters. He also ordered ashore a detachment of marines, plus two 9-pdr cannon and 18 muskets for distribution among the settlers. As the hostiles approached Seattle on January 26, the gunners aboard the *Decatur* fired solid shot, shells, and canister shot, which kept the attackers at bay. Meanwhile, Seattle residents and refugees from the surrounding area took shelter in the blockhouses. The village also teemed with dozens of friendly Native Americans, who crowded into the defile along the beach for protection.

In this painting by Emily Inez Denny, the eldest child of early settler David Denny, settlers are shown running to the North Blockhouse for safety during the attack on Seattle on January 26, 1856. The USS *Decatur* sits offshore in Elliott Bay, helping to protect the settlers from a threatened Native American attack. Denny was only three years old at the time of the battle, and was carried into the fort in her mother's arms. (Museum of History & Industry Collection, Seattle.)

F ATTACK ON THE BLOCKHOUSE AT FORT RAINES, WASHINGTON TERRITORY, 1856

On March 26, 1856, about 400 warriors of the Yakima, Klickitat, and Cascades people, who were unhappy with white encroachment on their land, attacked the settlers and a small detachment of military personnel at the Cascades of the Columbia River in Washington Territory. Burning most of the buildings in the small community, the hostiles laid siege to a blockhouse at the Middle Cascades called Fort Raines, in which both soldiers and civilians sought refuge. A relief force consisting of 40 dragoons commanded by Lieutenant Phil Sheridan, plus several howitzers, arrived aboard the steamer *Belle* from Fort Vancouver the following day and the hostiles were eventually driven off, leaving a total of 17 whites dead and 12 wounded along the entire length of the Cascades. The attack became known as the "Cascades Massacre" and was the costliest event in terms of casualties during the Yakima War of 1855–56.

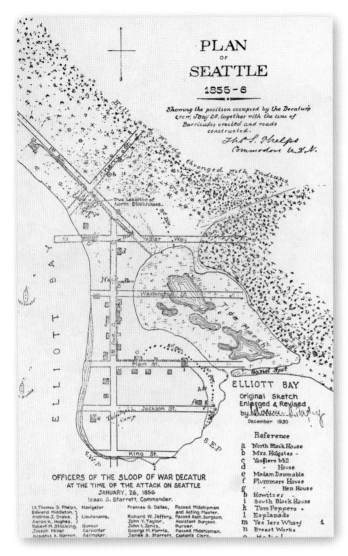

PLAN
OF
SEATTLE
1855-6

Showing the position occupied by the Decatur's crew, Jany 26, together with the line of Barricades erected and roads constructed.

Thos S. Phelps
Commodore U.S.N.

True Location of
North Blockhouse.

thronged with Indians

ELLIOTT BAY
Original Sketch
Enlarged & Revised
by
December 1930

Reference
a North Block House
b Mrs. Holgates "
c Yesflers Mill
d " House
e Madam Dermable
f Plummers House
g " Hen House
h Howitzer
i South Block House
k Tom Peppers "
l Esplanade
m Yes lers Wharf
n Breast Works

OFFICERS OF THE SLOOP OF WAR DECATUR
AT THE TIME OF THE ATTACK ON SEATTLE
JANUARY 26, 1856
Isaac S. Starrett, Commander.

Lt. Thomas S. Phelps,	Navigator	Frances G. Dallas,	Passed Midshipman and Acting Master.
Edward Middleton,			
Andrew J. Drake, } Lieutenants.		John Y. Taylor,	Assistant Surgeon.
Aaron K. Hughes, }		Richard W. Jeffery,	Passed Asst. Surgeon.
Robert M. Stocking, Gunner		John I. Jonas,	Purser.
Joseph Miller, Carpenter		George M. Morris,	Passed Midshipman.
Augustus A. Warren, Sailmaker		James S. Starrett,	Captain's Clerk.

From a sketch by Commodore Thomas Phelps at the time of the battle of Seattle in 1856, this map shows the position of the sloop USS *Decatur* and the *Brontes* barque in Elliott Bay. The location of breastworks built and defended by the US marines and seamen is also indicated at center left. The North Blockhouse at top left is incorrectly shown too far north of its true location, which was on a knoll at the waterfront about 600yds farther south on what is today Cherry Street. (University of Washington Libraries, Special Collections, UW4101)

Taking advantage of a lull in the firing around mid-morning, the settlers managed to evacuate their women and children to the USS *Decatur* and the *Brontes* barque, which had just arrived. Firing continued when the hostiles began setting fire to settlers' dwellings, but by nightfall they had been driven back. By the next morning they had gone, along with whatever settler stock, foodstuffs, and other property they could carry. Only two settlers had been killed, plus an unknown number of Native Americans.

Flowing through the Cascades Gorge, the Columbia River, in Oregon, was a major trade route to and from the West Coast, and greatly valued by Native Americans and European settlers. On March 26, 1856, a combined war party of Yakima, Klikitat, and Chinook braves led by Kamiakin attacked the white settlements at the Upper, Middle, and Lower Cascades. The day before, Colonel George Wright and three companies of the 9th Infantry had arrived via steamboat en route for The Dalles, leaving a sergeant and eight enlisted men to man a blockhouse called Fort Raines built to protect settlers at the Middle Cascades. Descending on the Lower Cascades, the hostiles destroyed a riverboat landing where a construction crew was building two bridges to accommodate a portage railroad. About 40 settlers at the Upper Cascades took refuge in a sturdy two-story storehouse, which the hostiles failed to burn down or capture. They also failed to trap the steamers *Mary* and *Wasco* above the rapids, and the crews, some of whom were wounded, got up steam and headed upriver to get help.

Meanwhile, at the Middle Cascades the hostiles besieged the Fort Raines blockhouse, named after Major Gabriel J. Raines, 4th Infantry, before 40 dragoons commanded by Lieutenant Phil Sheridan arrived from Fort Vancouver aboard the steamer *Belle* on March 27. Unable to reach the blockhouse, the dragoons withdrew after fierce fighting along the riverbank. The hostiles were finally driven off the next day following the arrival of further troops from Fort Walla Walla under Colonel Steptoe. Caught in a pincer movement between the forces of Sheridan and Steptoe, but alerted by the bugle calls of the latter, most of the Yakima escaped, leaving the Klikitat and Chinook braves to be captured. A total of 21 white defenders were killed or wounded. Nine of the captives, including Chief Chenoweth, were tried by a military commission and hanged after being found guilty of treason. After what became known as the "Cascades Massacre," the Army built a large blockhouse at the Upper Cascades called Fort Lugenbeel, and the smaller Fort Cascade at the lower rapids.

The Civil War period

With the onset of the Civil War in 1861, the US Army had to decide what to do with its forts in Washington Territory, Oregon, and California. The initial response was to close them, as they had no military purpose in the main context of the Civil War. However, as elements of the population in Oregon were strongly sympathetic toward the Confederacy, a Union presence there was felt prudent. Also, white settlers near reservations opposed closure of the forts, fearing a repeat of hostilities experienced in the 1850s. Thus, in the fall of 1861, the regular Army was replaced by volunteer citizen-soldiers from the West Coast. Continuing to serve as a depot and reserve station, Fort Vancouver was garrisoned by the 1st Washington Territory Infantry and the 1st Oregon Cavalry. An expedition from Fort Walla Walla during August 1862 quelled an uprising at the Umatilla Reservation led by the Native American prophet Tenounis, also known as the "Dreamer." This post also served as the base of operations during the Snake War of 1864 against the Northern Paiute, Bannock, and Western Shoshone bands who lived along the Snake River.

After delays caused by a very wet winter in southern California, the "California Column," commanded by Colonel James H. Carleton, set out from Fort Yuma in April 1862 to counter the Confederate threat in Arizona and New Mexico. As a result of sporadic fighting between miners and the Paiutes during the following year, elements of the 2nd California Cavalry established Camp Independence on Oak Creek in the Owens River Valley

Assigned to the 4th Infantry in 1855, 2nd Lieutenant Philip Sheridan commanded a detachment of 40 US dragoons during the operation to rescue civilians and soldiers besieged in the Fort Raines blockhouse at the Middle Cascades, Oregon Territory, in March 1856. He was wounded when a bullet grazed his nose during this action. (Library of Congress, USZ62-135919)

Photographed by Carleton E. Watkins in 1867 at the Upper Cascades, Oregon Territory, the blockhouse seen at right was known as Fort Lugenbeel and was built following the massacre at the Middle Cascades in 1856. The store and warehouse owned by the Bradford brothers stands at center, with the upper end of the portage facilities of the Oregon Steam Navigation Company at the water's edge to the right. (University of Washington Libraries, Special Collections Division)

Typical of the California volunteers that served in the West Coast fortifications during the Civil War, Private Thomas Smith wears the full dress uniform issued to the 1st through 5th California Volunteer Infantry in 1861. (Author's collection)

on the eastern slope of the Sierra Nevada Mountains. The first quarters at this post consisted of caves and crude huts hollowed out of a nearby ravine, but by the end of the year adobe barracks had been built. Expeditions from this post eventually forced the Native Americans to agree to peace talks in 1863, following which it was abandoned, only to be reoccupied after renewed hostilities in 1864.

Alcatraz Island served as the San Francisco Arsenal for the storage of firearms in order to prevent them falling into the hands of Southern sympathizers. It was also used to imprison deserters, insubordinate soldiers, and captured Confederates on the West Coast. In 1868 the Army established a permanent military prison on Alcatraz Island.

Providing an armed deterrent rather than seeing active service, over 500 artillerymen garrisoned Fort Point by 1865. The closest the fort ever came to seeing actual combat occurred after the end of the Civil War. During the summer of 1865 news reached San Francisco that the Confederate raider *Shenandoah* was off the California coast, and that the ship's commander, Captain James Waddell, was preparing her to run past the fort at night in order to turn her guns on the city. When he was only two days away from the Golden Gate, Waddell, who had been at sea for over a year, learned from a friendly British vessel of the surrender at Appomattox and abandoned his attack.

Later frontier wars

Unrest between the mining community and the Klamath people of northern California led to intermittent warfare after the Civil War, despite the treaty of 1864, which established the Klamath Reservation. In November 1867 a war party of about 100 Klamath warriors, led by a chief called "Colonel," attacked miners at Klamath Bluffs. When a detachment of Co. G, 9th Infantry, from Camp Lincoln, commanded by Lieutenant James M. Broome, came to their relief they found eight miners, plus some friendly Klamath from another tribe, besieged in a blockhouse and the hostiles "swaggering around with rifles, yagers [sic], shotguns, revolvers and their long knives." Following unsuccessful negotiations, Colonel ordered his warriors to withdraw, but tension remained and the blockhouse was again besieged in July 1868, when one miner was killed and another wounded.

The last major conflict between Native Americans and Europeans on the Pacific coast occurred in 1873 when the Modoc people of northern California refused to live on the same reservation as the Klamath, whom they considered to be their sworn enemy. During what became known as the Modoc War of 1873, troops from Fort Klamath and the Presidio of San Francisco converged on the Lava Beds on the border between California and Oregon

Territory in order to conduct an extended campaign against the Modoc hostiles, who were led by Kintpuash, also known as "Captain Jack." Meanwhile, panic spread among the civilian population. During the long campaign against the Modoc, troops operated in the Lava Beds from Camps Van Bremer and Wheaton.

Following defeat and capture on May 31, 1873, the Modoc were incarcerated in "a stockade of pine logs" at Fort Klamath. Visiting the post, a correspondent of the *San Francisco Bulletin* wrote: "The stockade is guarded by twenty-four men who stand watch and watch. Guards pace to and fro in front of the doors and along the raised platforms at the stockade corners." Responsible for the murder of General Edward Canby during armistice negotiations in April of that year, Captain Jack and three other Modoc leaders were hanged and buried at Fort Klamath on October 3, 1873. Following the Bannock War of 1879, which encroached on parts of eastern Oregon, Bannock and Paiute prisoners were held at Fort Harney and force-marched through knee-deep snow to Fort Simcoe, on the Yakima Reservation, and to Fort Vancouver, in Washington State, during the following year. By the fall of 1889, Fort Klamath was the last military frontier outpost in Oregon. With nearby settlers no longer in need of protection, the decision was made to close the fort. Following a harsh final winter with more than 20ft of snow, Co. I, 14th Infantry, marched out on June 23, 1890, and moved to Vancouver Barracks.

This gun crew was photographed by Eadweard Muybridge drilling with a mounted 15in. Rodman gun on Alcatraz Island during the 1860s. San Francisco can be seen in the distance. (Courtesy of The Bancroft Library)

THE FATE OF THE FORTS

The very nature of the building materials used guaranteed that virtually every trace of most of the original adobe-and-wood frontier forts of the West Coast would vanish within a few short years. The oldest federally designated park in Alaska, Sitka National Historical Park, was established as a federal park in 1890. It became a national monument in 1910 in order to commemorate the 1804 Battle of Sitka fought between the Tlingits and the Russians. All that remains of the Tlingit fort is a clearing at the site where it once stood. Although it had almost disappeared by 1841, the site of the Hudson's Bay Company Fort George/Astoria is now outlined in paint on sidewalks around 15th and Exchange Streets in Astoria, Oregon. A reconstructed bastion and the oldest gravestone in the Pacific Northwest are in a small park at the intersection in the same city. Fort Okanogan, in Washington State, was flooded in 1967 by the reservoir Lake Pateros because of the construction of the Wells Dam. Likewise, the original Fort Nez Perces, in Oregon, lies under the waters of the Columbia River. A plaque in downtown Walla Walla commemorates the location of the US Army Fort Walla Walla. Original buildings from the second fort of this name can still be found on the grounds of the Veteran Affairs Medical Center. The site of Sutter's Fort, in California, was bought by the "Native Sons of Golden West" in 1890. Donated to the state, it was restored to its supposed 1848 appearance commencing in 1947, as new details of its construction were uncovered.

Several blockhouses were dismantled and rebuilt elsewhere. The Alexander Blockhouse was moved to the modern city of Coupeville, the county seat of Island County, where it is preserved in the downtown area. What remained of Fort Yamhill, in Oregon, was sold by public auction in 1866. The blockhouse was so little desired by bidders that the auctioneer purchased it for $2.50 and left it on the site. After several years it was moved to the Grand Ronde Agency, where it was used as a jail and storehouse for nearly 40 years. Observing its deterioration, the citizens of Dayton lobbied to rescue and remove it to the Dayton City Park as a memorial to Joel Palmer, their most prominent citizen. The Yamhill Blockhouse was moved by horse-drawn wagons to Dayton on June 9, 1911, and re-erected the following year. It still stands there today. The original blockhouse, plus several other structures including the Royal Marine Cemetery, still occupies the site at English Camp on San Juan Island as part of the San Juan Island Historical Park maintained by the National Park Service.

Remaining in active service at the beginning of the 20th century, Fort Vancouver was expanded into Vancouver Barracks during World War I. During the interwar years, the 5th Infantry Brigade

In this portrait taken after his surrender, Kintpuash, or "Captain Jack," chief of the Modoc, wears the "striped calico shirt" issued to the prisoners at Fort Klamath. (US National Archives, NAA-43132)

Four Modoc leaders (Kintpuash, Black Jim, John Schonchin, and Boston Charley) were hanged by the US Army at Fort Klamath, Oregon, on October 3, 1873. Their graves are indicated by four wooden markers at the fort today. (Courtesy of the Fort Klamath Museum)

was based there, and for two years from 1936 it was commanded by future Army Chief of Staff George C. Marshall. Its final use was in World War II, when Vancouver Barracks was used as a staging area for troops embarking at Seattle. At this time the post enclosed 3,019 acres, and had billeting space for 250 officers and 7,295 enlisted personnel. Its days as an active military post came to an end in 1946, and it became a US National Monument in 1948, being redesignated as Fort Vancouver National Historic Site on June 30, 1961. In 1996, a 366-acre area around the fort, including Kanaka Village, the Columbia Barracks, and the bank of the river, was established as the Vancouver National Historic Reserve, in the care of the National Park Service.

In 1891, troopers of the 4th Cavalry based at the Presidio of San Francisco became the nation's first "park rangers" by patrolling the new Yosemite and Sequoia National Parks. Between 1898 and 1906, the Presidio of San Francisco served as the center for assembling, training, and transporting forces to the Philippine Islands during the Spanish–American War and subsequent Philippine–American War. The Letterman Army Hospital was modernized and expanded to care for the many wounded and seriously ill soldiers from these campaigns. The post repeated this role during World War II, the Korean War, and the Vietnam conflict.

In 1868 the post on Alcatraz Island became a detention facility for military prisoners. Among those incarcerated in its brick-built prison were some Hopi Native American men in the 1870s. The Spanish–American War increased the prison population from 26 to over 450, and after the 1906 San Francisco earthquake civilian prisoners were transferred to Alcatraz for safe confinement. On March 21, 1907, Alcatraz was officially designated as the "Western US Military Prison," which was changed to the "Pacific Branch, US Disciplinary Barracks" in 1915. From 1909–12, the Citadel was demolished down to the first floor, which was actually below ground level, to accommodate the new cell block that became the world's largest concrete prison, and remains the dominant feature on the island today. During World War I the prison held conscientious objectors, including Philip Grosser, who wrote a pamphlet entitled "Uncle Sam's Devil's Island" about his experiences there. The post was deactivated as a military prison in October 1933 and transferred to the Federal Bureau of Prisons, which modernized it into a maximum-security unit for high-risk civilian criminals during the following year.

Fort Point continued to serve as the "Guardian of the Golden Gate" during the years after the Civil War, and in 1882 was officially named Fort Winfield Scott after the famous hero from the Mexican War. However, as the name never caught on, it was later applied to an artillery post at the Presidio of San Francisco, and the original name continued in use. In 1892 the Army began constructing the new "Endicott System" of concrete fortifications armed with steel, breech-loading rifled guns, and within eight years all 103 of the smooth-bore cannon at Fort Point had been dismounted and sold for scrap. Moderately damaged in the 1906 earthquake, the fort was used over the next four decades as a barracks, for training, and for storage. Part of the interior wall was removed by the Army in 1913 as part of their short-lived attempt to convert it into a detention barracks. Soldiers from the 6th US Coast Artillery were stationed at the post during World War II in order to guard the minefields and the anti-submarine net that spanned the Golden Gate. During 1926 the American Institute of Architects proposed preserving Fort Point because of its outstanding military architecture, but funds were unavailable. Although plans for the construction of the Golden Gate Bridge in the 1930s called for the demolition of the fort, Chief Engineer Joseph Strauss redesigned the project in order to save it. Hence, the fort stands today directly below the southern approach to the bridge, underneath an arch that supports the roadway. Owing greatly to the work of the Fort Point Museum Association, established in 1959, the Fort Point National Historic Site was finally created in 1970.

THE FORTS TODAY

Although not exhaustive, this list includes the main frontier fort sites on the West Coast, owned by the National Park Service, government agencies, the local community, and those in private hands. At the time of writing, all of these sites are open to the public unless otherwise noted.

Alcatraz Island (Golden Gate National Recreational Area)
Location: San Francisco, California. Tours depart from Pier 33 (http://alcatrazcruises.com/).
Length of service: 1850–1934.
Description: brick-and-stone Citadel and barbette batteries.
Owner: National Park Service.
Relevant website: http://www.nps.gov/alca/index.htm

Fort Astoria/George (National Historic Landmark)
Location: Astoria, Oregon.
Length of service: 1811–25; 1830–48.
Description: nothing remains of the original site, although a small plot of land has been preserved and kept free of modern structures, and features a reconstructed bastion built in 1956.
Owner: City of Astoria.

Fort Clatsop (Lewis and Clark National Historical Park)
Location: near Warrenton, Oregon.

Length of service: December 1805 to March 1806.
Description: nothing remains of the original site. According to documentary evidence, the replica log buildings and picket wall are in need of reinterpretation.
Owner: National Park Service.
Relevant website: http://www.nps.gov/lewi/index.htm

Photographed from the southwest in 1934, Fort Point is dwarfed by the construction of the Golden Gate Bridge, which took about five years to complete. (Library of Congress, HABS CAL, 38-SANFRA, 4–1)

Fort Klamath

Location: near Klamath Falls, Oregon.
Length of service: 1863–90.
Description: log (later wood-frame) buildings around a parade ground. A replica of the log-built guardhouse serves as a museum today. The only remains of the original post are the graves of the four Modoc leaders who were tried and hanged there in 1873.
Owner: Fort Klamath Museum.
Relevant website: http://www.ohwy.com/or/f/ftklammu.htm

Fort Point National Historical Site (Golden Gate National Recreational Area)

Location: San Francisco, California.
Length of service: 1861–1926; 1941–45.
Description: brick-and-stone fort based on the "Third System" of military architecture.
Owner: National Park Service.
Relevant website: http://www.nps.gov/fopo/index.htm

Fort Ross State Historic Park
Location: off Highway 1, some 12 miles north of the hamlet of Jenner, California.
Length of service: 1812–41.
Description: replica stockade fort with the commandant's house the only surviving original structure.
Owner: California State.
Relevant website: http://www.parks.ca.gov/?page_id=449

Fort Steilacoom
Location: near Lakewood, Washington.
Length of service: 1849–68.
Description: log (later wood-frame-and-brick) buildings around a parade ground. Several of the latter survive today.
Owner: Historic Fort Steilacoom Association.
Relevant website: http://www.historicfortsteilacoom.com/index.php

Fort Stevens State Park
Location: near Womenton, Oregon.
Length of service: 1863–1947.
Description: earthwork battery, later concrete-and-steel gun fortifications.
Owner: Oregon State Parks.
Relevant website: http://www.oregonstateparks.org/park_179.php

Fort Vancouver National Historical Site
Location: Vancouver, Washington.
Length of service: Hudson's Bay Company fort, 1824–1860; Columbia Barracks, Fort Vancouver, or Vancouver Barracks, 1849–1946.
Description: stockade fort with bastion. Log-and-wood-frame buildings later built around a parade ground.
Owner: National Park Service.
Relevant website: http://www.nps.gov/fova/index.htm

Fort Yamhill State Heritage Site
Location: near Salem, Oregon.
Length of service: 1856.
Description: an original building surviving on the site is an officer's cottage once occupied by Lieutenant Philip Sheridan. A bastion was removed and eventually reconstructed in Dayton City Park, Oregon.
Owner: Oregon State Park.
Relevant website: http://www.oregonstateparks.org/park_254.php

Presidio of San Francisco (Golden Gate National Recreational Area)
Location: San Francisco, California.
Length of service: Spanish, 1776–1821; Mexican, 1821–46; US Army, 1846–1994.
Description: adobe, replaced by wood-frame and brick-and-stone.
Owner: National Park Service.
Relevant website: http://www.nps.gov/prsf/index.htm

Presidio of Monterey
Location: Monterey, California.

Length of service: Spanish, 1770–1822; Mexican, 1822–46; US Army, 1846 to the present day. The post now serves as the Defense Language Institute Foreign Language Center (DLIFLC).
Description: adobe, replaced by wood-frame and brick-and-stone.
Owner: US Government.
Relevant website: http://www.monterey.army.mil/about/about.html

Presidio of Santa Barbara (California State Parks)
Location: Santa Barbara, California.
Length of service: Spanish, 1782–1822; Mexican, 1822–46; US Army, 1846.
Description: adobe, much of which has been replicated since 1961.
Owner: Santa Barbara Trust for Historic Preservation.
Relevant website: http://www.sbthp.org/presidio.htm

San Juan Island National Historical Park
Location: Washington State Ferries depart for San Juan Island from the terminal at Anacortes, Washington.
Length of service: 1860–72.
Description: wooden blockhouse at English Camp at northern end of the island, and remains of an earthen redoubt at American Camp on the southern tip.
Owner: National Park Service.
Relevant website: http://www.nps.gov/fova/index.htm

Presidio of San Diego (National Historic Landmark)
Location: San Diego, California.
Length of service: Spanish, 1769–1822; Mexican, 1822–35.
Description: wood, followed by adobe, construction. The Serra Museum, adjacent the park, houses a collection of archeological artifacts related to the history of Spanish California.
Owner: National Park Service.
Relevant website: http://www.nps.gov/nr/travel/ca/ca2.htm

Sitka National Historical Park
Location: downtown Sitka, Alaska. Sitka is situated on Baranof Island on the outer coast of Alaska's Inside Passage. No roads reach the city from the mainland. Sitka can be reached only by air or sea. Visitors can travel to Sitka by scheduled and charter air services, ferries, and cruise ships.
Length of service: 1802–04.
Description: a clearing at the site where the Tlingit Fort once stood is all that remains.
Owner: National Park Service.
Relevant website: http://www.nps.gov/sitk/index.htm

Sutter's Fort State Historic Park
Location: Sacramento, California.
Length of service: 1840–c.1850s.
Description: adobe fort furnished and reconstructed to reflect its 1846 appearance.
Owner: Califoria State.
Relevant website: http://www.parks.ca.gov/?page_id=485

BIBLIOGRAPHY

Government reports

A Report of Barracks and Hospitals, with Descriptions of Military Posts, Circular No. 4., War Department, Surgeon General's Office, Government Printing Office (Washington, 1870)

A Report on the Hygiene of the United States Army, with Descriptions of Military Posts, Circular No. 8. War Department, Surgeon-General's Office, Government Printing Office (Washington, 1875)

Outline Description of U.S. Military Posts and Stations of the Year 1871, War Department, Quartermaster General's Office, Government Printing Office (Washington, 1872)

Reports of Explorations and Surveys for Pacific Railroad, Vol. 12, Book 1 (H. Ex. Doc. 56), Government Printing Office (Washington, 1860)

Revised Outline Descriptions of the Posts and Stations of Troops of the Military Division of the Pacific, commanded by Major-General John M. Schofield, Headquarters, San Francisco, Cal. (Washington, 1872)

Books

Brown, Frederick L., "Imagining Fort Clatsop" in *Oregon Historical Quarterly* (2006)

Emmons, George Thornton (ed. Frederica De Laguna), *The Tlingit Indians* (University of Washington Press: Seattle, 1991)

Frazer, Robert W., *Mansfield on the Condition of the Western Forts 1853–54* (University of Oklahoma Press: Norman, 1963)

Gray, William Henry, *A History of Oregon, 1792–1849, Drawn from Personal Observation and Authentic Information*, Harris & Holman: Portland, OR, 1870)

Hammond, John Martin, *Quaint and Historic Forts of North America* (Lippincott & Co.: Philadelphia, 1915)

Hussey, John A., *The History of Fort Vancouver and its Physical Structure* (Washington State Historical Society: Tacoma, 1957)

Inkersley, Arthur, *"Alexander Baranof and the Russian Colonies of America" in* Overland Monthly (Library Division, Provincial Archives of British Columbia, n.d.)

Kip, Lawrence, *Army Life on the Pacific* (Redfield: New York, 1859)

Langelier, John Phillip, & Daniel Bernard Rosen, Historic Resource Study: *El Presidio de San Francisco, a History under Spain and Mexico, 1776–1846* (National Park Service: Denver, 1992)

Lisiansky, Yuri, *A Voyage Around the World* (Booth & Longman: London, 1814)

Martini, John A., *Fort Point: Sentry at the Golden Gate* (Golden Gate National Park Association: San Francisco, 1991)

Nelson, H. B. (ed. P. E. Onstead), *A Webfoot Volunteer; The Diary of William M. Hilleary 1864–1866* (Oregon State University Press, Corvallis, 1965)

Prosch, Thomas W., "The Indian Wars in Washington Territory" in *The Quarterly of the Oregon Historical Society*, Vol. XVI, No. 1 (March 1915)

Ross, Alexander, *The Fur Hunters of the Far West* (The Lakeside Press: Chicago, 1924)

Scott, Robert N. (compiler), *The War of the Rebellion: A Compilation of the Official Records of the Union and Confederate Armies* (Washington, DC, 1880–1901)

Skott, Hilda, "The Run from Farm to Farm" in *Columbia Magazine*, Vol. 15, No. 3. (Fall 2001)

Thompson, Erwin N. and Sally B. Woodbridge, *Special History Study, Presidio of San Francisco: An Outline of Its Evolution as a U.S. Army Post, 1847–1990* (National Park Service: San Francisco, 1992)

Utley, Robert M. and Wilcomb E. Washburn, *The American Heritage History of the Indian Wars* (Simon and Schuster: New York, 1977)

Wilbur, Marguerite Eyer, (tr. and ed.), *A Pioneer at Sutter's fort, 1846–1850; the adventures of Heinrich Lienhard* (The Calafía Society: Los Angeles, 1941)

Newspapers

Alta California (San Francisco, California)

Weekly Oregonian (Portland, Oregon)

GLOSSARY

Bastion	A tower attached to the curtain wall of a fort.
Blockhouse	An independent strongpoint usually made of logs.
Ditch, or **dry moat**	This enclosed the walls of a stockade, stone-built fort, or brick-built fort.
Embrasure	Originally the name for the gap between merlons, by the 19th century this referred to an aperture through which cannon fired.
Gallery	An outdoor roofed balcony used for patrolling the walls of a fort.
Merlon	Solid part of the crenellation on the parapet of a fortress wall.
Redoubt	An enclosed defensive emplacement outside a larger fortification, usually consisting of earthworks, although some were constructed of stone or brick.
Sally port	Well-defended entrance or door in a fortification designed for the quick passage of troops who might sally out to attack a besieging enemy.
Stockade, palisade, or picketed wall	Log-built curtain wall protecting a fort.

INDEX